Book 2 – Ages 10-11

Lay the groundwork for unparalleled success in the 11+ English comprehension and Verbal Reasoning exams with our 11+ Vocabulary builder.

Key Features:

- Oxford 3000™ Aligned: 750 essential words, carefully selected from the esteemed Oxford English Corpus, ensuring that you're equipped with high-frequency words that you're most likely to encounter in your educational journey.

- Simple Definitions & Examples: For each word, we provide a simple synonym for easy recall, along with an age-appropriate and easy-to-grasp explanation. Only knowing a one-word explain is sufficient to better answer questions on most tests.

- Short Sharp Examples: We provide two example sentences with every word that provides some context for quicker learning and understanding. A third sentence is used as part of the word bank tests.

- Designed for Self-Study: Manageable chunks with a weekly structure for independent learners to prevent overwhelm. With three progressively challenging tests accompanying every word and a fun weekly word riddle, you'll cement your knowledge and track your progress effortlessly.

- Stepping Stone to Excellence: Our books use a proven vocabulary-building system. Key words are tested repeatedly, ensuring deep learning and improved performance on English and Verbal Reasoning tests. Book 1 in the series is aimed at ages 9-10, and Book 2 for ages 10-11. Compatible with all exam boards.

Learn more about our other publications at www.bgsbooks.com

Edition 1.0 – May 2024

ISBN: 978-1-7394318-4-6

Contact:

BGS Books Ltd
Office 3504
58 Peregrine Road
Hainault, IG6 3SZ

Tel: 0333 339 5747

Sales & General Enquiries: info@bgsbooks.com

Support Enquiries: **WhatsApp** your query to:
 +44 333 339 5747 or use the QR code shown.

WhatsApp

How to use this book

Week Number

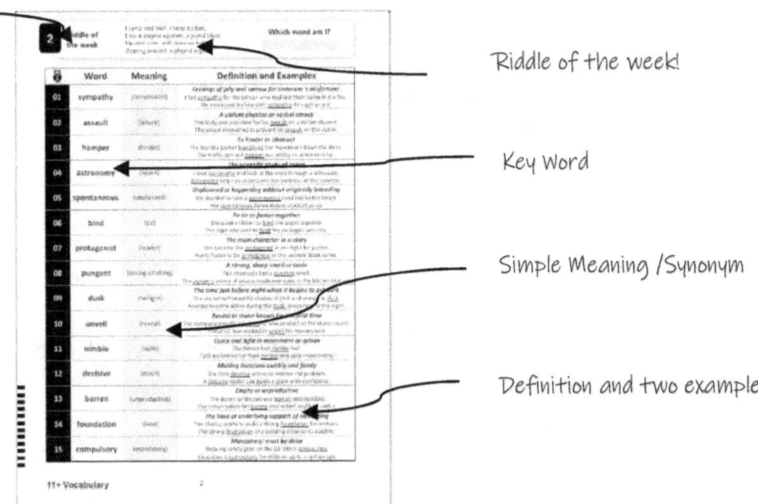

Riddle of the week!

Key Word

Simple Meaning /Synonym

Definition and two examples

1 First, aim to learn 3 words per day. There are 15 words per page. We suggest weekly units of 5 days. For each word, memorise the corresponding 1-word meaning/synonym.

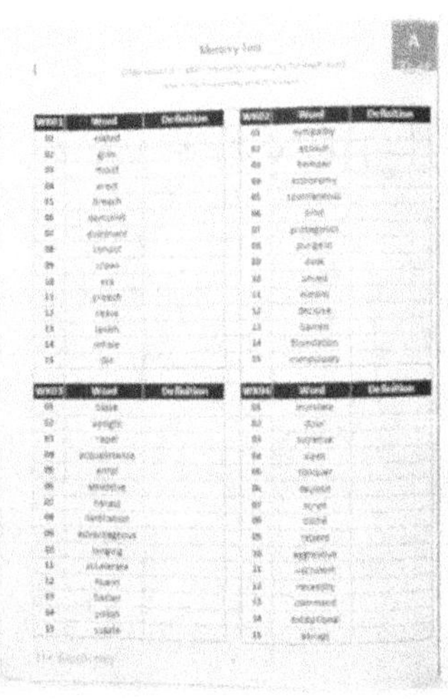

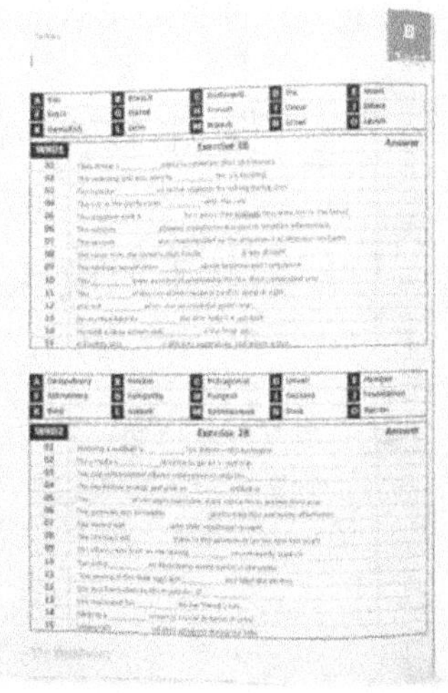

2 Next, take a memory recall test each week. Write down the 1 word meaning next to each word.

3 To ensure the you have understood the meaning of each word, take the next test B. Select a word from the weeks word bank to complete the sentence.

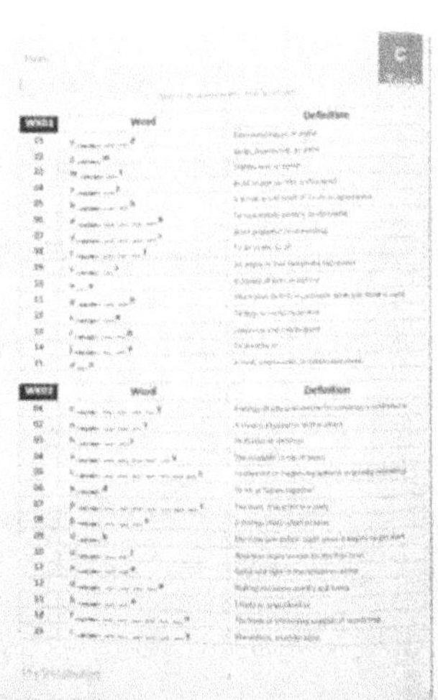

4 Test C should be taken 2-3 weeks after Test B. Read the definitions then complete the root word. The first and last letters are provided as a clue.

5 Finally – keep track of the scores as every unit of 15 words can be tested in different ways up to 3x!

Table of Contents

I push things back, a later date,
A change of plans, a chance to wait.
Events must shift, a small delay,
I give you time another day.

Which word am I?

	Word	Meaning	Definition and Examples
01	**futile**	(useless)	***Pointless, having no effect*** Any attempt to change his mind would be <u>futile</u>. Don't waste time on <u>futile</u> pursuits.
02	**mimic**	(copy)	***To imitate or copy the actions of someone or something*** The comedian was known for <u>mimicking</u> celebrities. Parrots are known to <u>mimic</u> human speech.
03	**protract**	(prolong)	***To prolong for an unnecessarily long time*** The illness <u>protracted</u> his recovery, keeping him bedridden for longer. He <u>protracted</u> the meeting by repeatedly bringing up irrelevant topics.
04	**crisis**	(hurry)	***A severe problem or danger needing urgent attention*** A natural disaster can trigger a humanitarian crisis. The sudden illness plunged the family into crisis.
05	**confer**	(discuss or grant)	***To discuss in order to reach a decision*** The teacher <u>conferred</u> with the student's parents. The university will <u>confer</u> degrees upon the graduating students.
06	**discernible**	(noticeable)	***Able to be noticed or understood*** A <u>discernible</u> shift in the wind hinted at a storm. The difference in colour was barely <u>discernible</u>.
07	**fervour**	(passion)	***Intense and passionate feeling*** He spoke with great <u>fervour</u> about the cause he believed in. The fans showed great <u>fervour</u> by cheering loudly for their team.
08	**decadent**	(luxury)	***Luxurious, indulgent, or excessively rich*** They lived a <u>decadent</u> lifestyle. The chocolate cake was <u>decadent</u> and rich.
09	**terrain**	(landscape)	***A stretch of land, especially with regard to its physical features*** The rocky <u>terrain</u> of the mountain made the hike very challenging. The lunar <u>terrain</u> is covered in craters.
10	**hurtle**	(rush)	***Move very quickly and often uncontrollably*** The motorcycle <u>hurtled</u> down the road at high speed. The roller coaster will <u>hurtle</u> down the track at high speeds.
11	**savoury**	(non-sweet)	***Of food: salty or spicy, not sweet*** I love <u>savoury</u> snacks like pretzels and chips! We enjoyed a <u>savoury</u> meal at the restaurant.
12	**constant**	(continuous)	***Happening all the time or repeatedly*** He has been a <u>constant</u> source of support. The ticking clock was a <u>constant</u> sound in the room.
13	**postpone**	(delay)	***Delay until later*** We had to <u>postpone</u> the picnic because of the rain. Don't <u>postpone</u> important tasks.
14	**philosophical**	(thoughtful)	***Relating to the study of wisdom and knowledge*** She had a very <u>philosophical</u> outlook on life. She pondered <u>philosophical</u> questions about the universe.
15	**nemesis**	(adversary)	***A long-standing rival or enemy*** Bad habits can be a person's worst <u>nemesis</u>. In the story, the hero faced his <u>nemesis</u> in a final battle.

11+ Vocabulary

A weight upon the troubled heart,
A pain so deep, it tears apart.
Despair and sorrow fill my mind,
A torment that I cannot find.

Which word am I?

	Word	Meaning	Definition and Examples
01	**wrath**	(anger)	***Extreme anger*** The dragon unleashed its <u>wrath</u> on the village. The king's <u>wrath</u> was feared by all who dared to defy his authority.
02	**cathartic**	(relieving)	***Releasing strong emotions in a cleansing way*** A good cry can be <u>cathartic</u>. Writing in a journal can be <u>cathartic</u> and help express feelings.
03	**mournful**	(sorrowful)	***Expressing sorrow or grief*** The song had a sad, <u>mournful</u> sound. The <u>mournful</u> sound of the bagpipes filled the air.
04	**clamour**	(noise)	***Loud and persistent noise, often with shouting*** People made a lot of noise with their <u>clamour</u>. The <u>clamour</u> of the crowd could be heard from a distance.
05	**unprecedented**	(never before)	***Never done or known before*** The storm was of <u>unprecedented</u> strength and caused a lot of damage. The scale of the natural disaster was <u>unprecedented</u>.
06	**compliance**	(obey)	***The act of following rules or commands*** Anyone who didn't <u>comply</u> with the rules would be expelled. His <u>compliance</u> with the rules was admirable.
07	**shrewd**	(clever)	***Having sharp powers of judgment*** The <u>shrewd</u> negotiator secured a favourable deal for his client. She was <u>shrewd</u> and didn't tell anyone how much she was revising.
08	**slum**	(poor)	***A poor, overcrowded urban area*** Many people lived in poverty in the crowded <u>slum</u>. The overcrowded <u>slum</u> lacked basic sanitation.
09	**flippant**	(disrespectful)	***Not serious, showing a lack of respect*** She regretted her <u>flippant</u> attitude. His <u>flippant</u> remarks about the serious topic offended others.
10	**ration**	(portion)	***A fixed amount of something allowed, especially in short supply*** They had to <u>ration</u> their water supply as there was a drought. During the war, families had to <u>ration</u> their food.
11	**despise**	(hate)	***Hate strongly*** I <u>despise</u> lying, bullies and cruelty. He <u>despised</u> the taste of brussels sprouts and refused to eat them.
12	**insurmountable**	(difficult)	***Impossible to overcome*** The task seemed <u>insurmountable</u>, but they were determined. Don't be discouraged by <u>insurmountable</u> obstacles.
13	**cringe**	(embarrass)	***Feel embarrassed or disgusted*** Her rude comments made everyone <u>cringe</u>. I <u>cringe</u> when I remember my awkward moments.
14	**meander**	(wander)	***To follow a winding path*** The creek <u>meanders</u> all through the woods. The river would <u>meander</u> through the valley, creating scenic views.
15	**anguish**	(pain)	***Extreme suffering and distress*** Losing her beloved dog caused the girl a lot of <u>anguish</u>. The news caused her great <u>anguish</u>.

My face reveals no hint of smile,
Unbending will, a rigid style.
I may rebuke with words so sharp,
A chilling look, my spirit's harp.

Which word am I?

	Word	Meaning	Definition and Examples
01	comrade	(friend)	***A close friend*** Comrades are good friends or people who share a common goal. My hiking buddy is my most trusted comrade.
02	stern	(strict)	***Strict and severe*** He received a stern warning from his boss. The teacher's stern warning silenced the misbehaving students.
03	ambassador	(representative)	***A person representing their country or a cause*** The ambassador represented our country abroad. He acted as an ambassador for peace.
04	heritage	(legacy)	***Cultural traditions or features passed down from the past*** He was proud of his family's rich cultural heritage. Preserving our cultural heritage is essential for future generations.
05	coalition	(alliance)	***A temporary group formed for a goal*** A coalition of countries joined the fight. The friends formed a coalition to try and win the contest.
06	narrative	(story)	***A story or account of events*** The author wrote a compelling narrative about her childhood. He spun a wild narrative about his adventures.
07	correlate	(linked)	***To have a close connection between two things*** Researchers found a strong correlation between smoking and illness. Good sleep habits correlate with better health.
08	detractors	(critics)	***People who criticize something strongly*** Don't let your detractors discourage you. Despite detractors, the artist continued to pursue their passion.
09	antiquated	(outdated)	***Outdated or no longer in use*** The old typewriter with its manual keys seemed quite antiquated. The computer system was antiquated and needed an upgrade.
10	predominantly	(mainly)	***Mainly or mostly*** The club was predominantly made up of girls. The forest is predominantly populated by tall pine trees.
11	albeit	(although)	***Although or even though*** We got lost on the trail, but albeit a little late, we still found our way. She enjoyed the party, albeit it was a bit noisy.
12	indispensable	(essential)	***Absolutely necessary*** A good dictionary is an indispensable tool for a writer. Water is indispensable for survival.
13	community	(people)	***People living in a shared area*** The blogger built a large online community of followers. A strong sense of community helps build a supportive environment.
14	sarcasm	(mockery)	***The use of irony to mock or convey contempt*** Sometimes, it's hard to tell if she's using sarcasm or being serious. Sarcasm can be hurtful if used excessively.
15	void	(empty)	***Completely empty; invalid*** The judge declared the contract void because it wasn't signed. The room felt strangely void of any furniture.

11+ Vocabulary

🦉	Word	Meaning	Definition and Examples
01	**plethora**	(abundance)	***A large or excessive amount of something*** There is a <u>plethora</u> of information available online. The buffet offered a <u>plethora</u> of delicious options for dinner.
02	**fiend**	(demon)	***An evil or wicked person*** The villain in the movie was a cruel <u>fiend</u>. The witch in the fairy tale was portrayed as a <u>fiend</u>.
03	**premature**	(early)	***Happening too soon, before the proper time*** It's <u>premature</u> to celebrate before we know the final score. The flowers bloomed <u>prematurely</u> due to the unseasonably weather.
04	**transpire**	(occur)	***To occur or happen*** We waited impatiently to see what would <u>transpire</u> next in the story. We will never know exactly how the incident <u>transpired</u>.
05	**dearth**	(scarce)	***A scarcity or lack of something*** There's a <u>dearth</u> of affordable houses in our area. The region experienced a <u>dearth</u> of rainfall, leading to drought.
06	**diverse**	(varied)	***Showing a lot of variety*** The city was very <u>diverse</u>, with people from many different cultures. The forest is home to a <u>diverse</u> range of plant and animal species.
07	**terse**	(concise)	***Brief and to the point*** His <u>terse</u> reply made me think he was angry. His response was <u>terse</u>, consisting of only a few words.
08	**contention**	(dispute)	***A disagreement or conflict*** There was <u>contention</u> between neighbours over the broken fence. The siblings had a <u>contention</u> about who gets the bigger room.
09	**stoic**	(unemotional)	***Enduring hardship without showing emotion*** He remained <u>stoic</u> in the face of difficulty. Despite the challenges, the <u>stoic</u> soldier continued to fulfil his duty.
10	**ardour**	(eager)	***Enthusiasm or passion*** His <u>ardour</u> for learning was contagious. The artist painted with great <u>ardour</u> and dedication.
11	**vivid**	(colourful)	***Bright and distinct; producing strong mental images*** He had a <u>vivid</u> dream that felt very real. The memory of her holiday was still <u>vivid</u> in her mind after many years.
12	**rancid**	(foul)	***Smelling or tasting unpleasant*** The <u>rancid</u> odour coming from the trash made them gag. The <u>rancid</u> smell of spoiled milk filled the kitchen.
13	**cordial**	(friendly)	***Warm and friendly*** The host greeted us with a <u>cordial</u> smile. The neighbours exchanged <u>cordial</u> greetings every morning.
14	**immerse**	(submerge)	***To completely cover in liquid, or to deeply involve oneself*** She <u>immersed</u> herself in her studies. The artist would <u>immerse</u> himself in his work for hours at a time.
15	**adulation**	(admire)	***Excessive praise or admiration*** The popstar received a lot of <u>adulation</u> from her fans. Excessive <u>adulation</u> can lead to arrogance.

🦉	Word	Meaning	Definition and Examples
01	delectable	(delicious)	***Delightful, especially of food*** Delectable food tastes simply delicious. The cake was delectable, and everyone wanted more.
02	predecessor	(ancestor)	***A person who held a job or office before the current person*** The new mayor aims to build upon the work of her predecessor. The new phone model is far superior to its predecessor.
03	incorporate	(merge)	***Include as a part of something larger*** They decided to incorporate feedback into the next design. The chef decided to incorporate new ingredients into the recipe.
04	nuance	(subtlety)	***A subtle difference or variation*** He appreciated the nuanced flavours of the wine. There's a nuance in the way she smiles that shows her true feelings.
05	perturbed	(disturbed)	***Disturbed, feeling anxious or unsettled*** Their bad behaviour perturbed the teacher. She was perturbed by the strange noises.
06	decree	(order)	***An official order or decision*** The judge's decree settled the legal dispute. The king issued a decree declaring a holiday.
07	degrade	(humiliate)	***Treat with disrespect or make worse*** Don't degrade yourself by engaging in cruel behaviour. Bullying can degrade a person's self-esteem.
08	ecstatic	(overjoyed)	***Feeling extreme happiness*** The child was ecstatic when she opened her birthday presents. Winning the championship made them ecstatic with excitement.
09	duplicity	(two-faced)	***Deceitfulness or double-dealing*** The spy's duplicity allowed him to gather information from both sides. His duplicity was revealed when his lies were exposed.
10	taint	(contaminate)	***To contaminate or pollute something*** The scandal tainted the politician's reputation. The factory's emissions began to taint the air and water.
11	shove	(push)	***To push forcefully*** Don't shove your brother! The crowded train station led to people having to shove to get on.
12	rudimentary	(basic)	***Basic or undeveloped*** His first attempts at drawing were very rudimentary. The early computers had rudimentary features compared to today.
13	prudent	(wise)	***Wise, careful in making decisions*** It's prudent to save for retirement. It's prudent to save money for unexpected expenses.
14	lucid	(clear)	***Clear and easy to understand*** Even though the subject was difficult, my teacher made it very lucid. The teacher's explanations were lucid, making complex concepts simple.
15	circulate	(distribute)	***To move around or spread*** Please circulate this email to the entire team. The rumour began to circulate around the school.

11+ Vocabulary

I bring no danger, cause no strife,
A gentle touch on threads of life.
Though growth may come, no fear takes hold,
My presence kind, a story told.

Which word am I?

	Word	Meaning	Definition and Examples
01	stampede	(rush)	***A sudden rush of panicked animals or people*** A stampede of wild horses charged across the field. The loud noise caused a stampede among the frightened animals.
02	pivotal	(crucial)	***Crucially important*** Winning the championship was a pivotal moment in his career. The discovery of a cure was pivotal in the fight against the disease.
03	miserly	(frugal)	***Hoarding money and reluctant to spend*** The miserly old man refused to spend any of his money. Don't be miserly; share your snacks with your sister.
04	pillage	(plunder)	***Stealing violently, especially in a time of war*** The pirates would pillage villages for treasures. Vandals pillaged the abandoned house.
05	disarray	(disorder)	***Disorder or confusion*** The sudden news threw her plans into disarray. The room was in a state of disarray after the children played.
06	gregarious	(sociable)	***Sociable and enjoying the company of others*** She was a gregarious person who loved parties. Some animals are gregarious and live in groups.
07	palpable	(tangible)	***So intense it's almost physically felt*** Her excitement before the concert was palpable. The tension in the room was so palpable that you could almost touch it.
08	malevolent	(malicious)	***Having ill intentions or wishing harm upon others*** Spreading malevolent rumours can cause great harm. The villain's malevolent laughter echoed through the dark castle.
09	concept	(idea)	***An idea or understanding*** The architect presented her concept for the new building. The concept of time is essential for organizing our lives.
10	essence	(base)	***The fundamental nature or most important quality of something*** The essence of her message was about kindness. The essence of a good friendship is trust and understanding.
11	benign	(harmless)	***Gentle or kind; not harmful*** He had a benign and gentle nature. A benign smile reassured everyone that there was nothing to fear.
12	harbour	(shelter)	***A port, or a place of shelter & safety*** The ships took shelter in the harbour during the storm. The small cove will harbour boats during the storm.
13	ravenous	(hungry)	***Extremely hungry*** I was ravenous after playing soccer all day. After a long hike, they were ravenous and eagerly devoured the meal.
14	articulate	(well spoken)	***Able to express ideas clearly and fluently*** The speaker was very articulate and easy to understand. He sent an articulate and well-written email.
15	finesse	(skill)	***Skilful and delicate handling of a situation*** She handled the difficult situation with great finesse. The pianist played the difficult piece with finesse and precision.

With rules and facts, I love to bore,
The smallest detail, I must explore.
My focus narrows, my words so neat,
Trivial errors make me incomplete.

Which word am I?

	Word	Meaning	Definition and Examples
01	scorn	(disdain)	*The feeling that someone or something is worthless or despicable* She looked at her messy brother with <u>scorn</u>. The arrogant character treated everyone with disdain and <u>scorn</u>.
02	verdict	(decision)	*Decision e.g. On a court case* The public's <u>verdict</u> on the movie was mixed. The jury reached a <u>verdict</u> of guilty.
03	alleviate	(relieve)	*Make pain or suffering less severe* Taking medicine helped <u>alleviate</u> my headache pain. Medicine can help <u>alleviate</u> the symptoms of a cold.
04	exhibit	(display)	*Show something publicly (like in a museum)* The museum will <u>exhibit</u> a collection of rare artifacts. He didn't <u>exhibit</u> any signs of the illness.
05	surpass	(exceed)	*Exceed or be greater than* Her achievements <u>surpassed</u> everyone else's in the class. The latest technology <u>surpasses</u> anything we've seen before.
06	tenacity	(persistence)	*The quality of being determined or persistent* It took great <u>tenacity</u> for her to complete the marathon. The climber's <u>tenacity</u> allowed him to reach the summit.
07	congregation	(assembly)	*A group of people gathered for religious worship* We watched a <u>congregation</u> gather for prayers. The <u>congregation</u> gathered for the church service.
08	incidence	(occurrence)	*The occurrence or frequency of something* The <u>incidence</u> of the disease has decreased in recent years. The <u>incidence</u> of flu increases during the winter months.
09	pedantic	(nitpicky)	*Excessively concerned with minor details or rules* The teacher was <u>pedantic</u>, always focusing on tiny grammar errors. Don't be <u>pedantic</u> and focus on minor details.
10	proliferation	(increase)	*Rapid increase in number* The <u>proliferation</u> of smartphones changed how people communicate. The <u>proliferation</u> of rabbits caused problems for farmers.
11	gauge	(measure)	*Measure or estimate* It's difficult to <u>gauge</u> his reaction. Use a tire <u>gauge</u> to check the air pressure in your car tires.
12	negligent	(careless)	*Failing to take care* It was <u>negligent</u> of him to leave the campfire unattended. <u>Negligent</u> driving can lead to accidents.
13	impartial	(unbiased)	*Fair, not taking sides* It's hard to remain <u>impartial</u> in a conflict between friends. An <u>impartial</u> judge ensures a fair trial for both sides.
14	rind	(peel)	*The tough outer layer or skin of certain fruits or cheeses* He carefully removed the <u>rind</u> from the watermelon. The orange <u>rind</u> adds flavour to the zest used in cooking and baking.
15	arbitrary	(random)	*Unfairly chosen; based on chance rather than reason* The teacher's decision about seating seemed <u>arbitrary</u>; it felt unfair. He had an <u>arbitrary</u> way of assigning tasks.

11+ Vocabulary

	Word	Meaning	Definition and Examples
01	chronological	(in order)	**Arranged in the order things happened** The events were listed in <u>chronological</u> order. A <u>chronological</u> timeline helps understand historical events in sequence.
02	campaign	(plan)	**A series of actions to achieve a goal** He launched a political <u>campaign</u> for mayor. They launched a <u>campaign</u> to raise awareness.
03	saturate	(soak or excessive)	**Soak thoroughly or fill until no more can be absorbed** The market is <u>saturated</u> with too many similar products. The heavy rain started to <u>saturate</u> the ground, creating puddles.
04	supplement	(addition)	**Something added to complete a thing** I take a vitamin <u>supplement</u> to make sure I get enough nutrients. She <u>supplements</u> her income with a part-time job.
05	renowned	(famous)	**Famous and well-known** The city is <u>renowned</u> for its beautiful architecture. The artist became <u>renowned</u> for their unique and innovative style.
06	sceptical	(unconvinced)	**Not easily convinced; having doubts or reservations** I was <u>sceptical</u> about the promises in the advertisement. She had a <u>sceptical</u> attitude towards new ideas.
07	submerge	(beneath)	**Go beneath the surface of water** The submarine <u>submerged</u> underwater. Divers can <u>submerge</u> themselves underwater for extended periods.
08	candour	(honest)	**The quality of being honest and open** His <u>candour</u> and honesty were refreshing. Candour is <u>important</u> for building trust in relationships.
09	gung-ho	(enthusiasm)	**Enthusiastic and eager** He was <u>gung-ho</u> about starting the new project. The team was <u>gung-ho</u> about winning the championship.
10	phenomenon	(occurrence)	**A remarkable fact or occurrence** The Northern Lights are a beautiful natural <u>phenomenon</u>. The solar eclipse is a natural <u>phenomenon</u> that occurs periodically.
11	pitfall	(trap)	**A hidden or unsuspected danger or difficulty** There are many <u>pitfalls</u> to avoid when starting a business. One of the <u>pitfalls</u> of social media is cyberbullying.
12	resolution	(determination)	**A firm decision to do or not to do something** My New Year's <u>resolution</u> is to exercise more. The conflict reached a peaceful <u>resolution</u>.
13	overwhelming	(overpowering)	**Intense and difficult to resist** Sometimes homework can feel <u>overwhelming</u> when there's too much. The support from the community was <u>overwhelming</u>.
14	persona	(identity)	**The image a person presents to the public** The pop star created a cool and edgy <u>persona</u> for her stage act. On stage, the actor adopts a different <u>persona</u> from their everyday self.
15	potent	(powerful)	**Having a strong effect or influence** It was a <u>potent</u> symbol of hope and resilience. The medicine proved to be <u>potent</u> in treating the illness.

	Word	Meaning	Definition and Examples
01	enclosure	(area)	*An area surrounded by a fence or barrier* The animals live in a large <u>enclosure</u> at the zoo. The zoo's lion <u>enclosure</u> keeps the animals safely contained.
02	predicament	(trouble)	*A difficult, unpleasant, or embarrassing situation* The lost hikers were in a dangerous <u>predicament</u>. She was in a <u>predicament</u> when she realized she had lost her wallet.
03	emanate	(originate)	*Come from a source (light, smell, etc.)* A warm glow seemed to <u>emanate</u> from the fireplace. A soothing melody seemed to <u>emanate</u> from the piano.
04	profession	(occupation)	*A paid job that requires specialized training* Teaching is a <u>profession</u> that shapes the minds of future generations. Medicine is a respected and noble <u>profession</u>.
05	incite	(provoke)	*Encourage or provoke someone to do something, often violent* His speech was designed to <u>incite</u> the crowd to violence. The coach tried to <u>incite</u> the team with an inspiring speech.
06	maverick	(rebel)	*An independent person, not following the usual way* That scientist is a <u>maverick</u> for coming up with such a wild new invention. The <u>maverick</u> artist challenged traditional artistic norms.
07	oblige	(compel)	*To do something as a favour or to meet a request* She was happy to <u>oblige</u> and help her friend with the project. Can you <u>oblige</u> by helping me carry these books?
08	curt	(abrupt)	*Rudely brief or abrupt* He ended the conversation with a <u>curt</u> goodbye. His response was <u>curt</u>, lacking politeness.
09	residue	(leftover)	*What's left behind after removing the main part* Baking cookies left a sticky <u>residue</u> on the countertop. The <u>residue</u> left on the glass indicated a thorough cleaning was needed.
10	disparage	(mean)	*Criticize or speak badly of someone* She tried to <u>disparage</u> her opponent's reputation. It's not polite to <u>disparage</u> others based on their appearance.
11	overt	(obvious)	*Done or shown openly* His feelings were <u>overt</u>; everyone could see he was upset. The sign was <u>overt</u> and easy to read.
12	solitude	(isolation)	*Being alone; without company* Sometimes it's nice to spend time in <u>solitude</u> and reflect. After a busy day, he craved <u>solitude</u>.
13	condemn	(disapprove)	*To express strong disapproval or criticize severely* The old building was <u>condemned</u> and scheduled for demolition. The chief <u>condemned</u> the person who started the fire.
14	spendthrift	(wasteful)	*Someone who spends money wastefully* The <u>spendthrift</u> blew all his money on frivolous things. The <u>spendthrift</u> quickly exhausted their savings on luxury items.
15	sporadic	(irregular)	*Occurring occasionally or irregularly* We received <u>sporadic</u> reports of UFO sightings in the area. The <u>sporadic</u> rainfall was not enough to alleviate the drought conditions.

11+ Vocabulary

	Word	Meaning	Definition and Examples
01	monotonous	(tedious)	***Dull and repetitive*** His job was <u>monotonous</u>; he did the same thing every day. The <u>monotonous</u> sound of the clock ticking made him sleepy.
02	forsake	(abandon)	***To abandon or give up on someone or something*** She had to <u>forsake</u> her hobbies due to work. Friends should not <u>forsake</u> each other in times of need.
03	accumulate	(gather)	***To gather or collect over time*** I tend to <u>accumulate</u> way too many toys! Saving a little money each week will <u>accumulate</u> over time.
04	tangible	(touchable)	***Perceptible by touch, real or concrete*** We need <u>tangible</u> proof to solve this mystery. The success of the project was <u>tangible</u> through increased sales.
05	truant	(absent)	***A student absent from school without permission*** The <u>truant</u> student skipped school to go to the park. He played <u>truant</u> and went to the movies.
06	encompass	(include)	***To surround or include*** The book <u>encompasses</u> the entire history of the country. The forest will <u>encompass</u> various types of trees and wildlife.
07	certify	(confirm)	***To confirm or guarantee something is true*** The doctor <u>certified</u> that she was fit to return to work. A certificate can <u>certify</u> your completion of a course.
08	precarious	(unstable)	***Unstable, likely to fall or collapse*** The stack of plates balanced <u>precariously</u> on the table. Climbing the rickety ladder felt <u>precarious</u>, so she decided not to.
09	venture	(attempt)	***A risky journey or undertaking*** They decided to <u>venture</u> into the unknown forest. The entrepreneur decided to <u>venture</u> into selling computers.
10	profligate	(wasteful)	***Recklessly extravagant or wasteful*** His <u>profligate</u> spending habits got him into debt. He warned against the <u>profligate</u> use of time
11	affinity	(liking)	***A natural liking or connection*** I have a strong <u>affinity</u> for dogs; I just love them! They had an <u>affinity</u> for the same type of music.
12	annihilated	(destroyed)	***Completely destroyed or wiped out*** The entire city was <u>annihilated</u> by the earthquake. The hurricane almost <u>annihilated</u> the small village.
13	labyrinth	(maze)	***A complex and confusing network of passages*** The garden featured an elaborate maze that was like a <u>labyrinth</u>. The maze was a <u>labyrinth</u> of twists and turns.
14	perpetuate	(continue)	***To cause something to continue indefinitely*** Repeating rumours only <u>perpetuates</u> them. Old traditions can <u>perpetuate</u> outdated views.
15	languish	(weaken)	***To become weak or feeble*** The prisoner <u>languished</u> in jail for years. Without sunlight, plants may <u>languish</u> and wilt.

	Word	Meaning	Definition and Examples
01	infuse	(instil)	***Fill something with a quality*** They <u>infused</u> the tea with the flavour of herbs. Her kindness <u>infused</u> the room with a warm atmosphere.
02	readily	(easily)	***Easily, quickly, and willingly*** My dog <u>readily</u> fetches the ball whenever I throw it. The experienced chef could prepare a delicious meal <u>readily</u>.
03	strut	(walk arrogantly)	***To walk with a proud, confident manner*** The peacock <u>strutted</u> around, showing off its feathers. The model <u>strutted</u> down the runway.
04	compromise	(agreement)	***An agreement where each side gives in a bit*** They <u>compromised</u> their safety by ignoring the warning signs. Negotiation often involves finding a <u>compromise</u>.
05	mitigate	(lessen)	***To make less severe or harsh*** Wearing a helmet can help <u>mitigate</u> the risk of a head injury. Planting trees can help <u>mitigate</u> the effects of climate change.
06	attribute	(a feature)	***A quality or characteristic*** He <u>attributed</u> his success to hard work and determination. One positive <u>attribute</u> of a good leader is empathy.
07	deride	(mock)	***To mock or ridicule*** The bullies <u>derided</u> the other children. Critics <u>derided</u> the film as unoriginal.
08	deject	(sad)	***To make someone feel sad or hopeless*** The gloomy weather made me feel <u>dejected</u>. Failing the test can <u>deject</u> a student.
09	contrary	(opposite)	***The opposite*** <u>Contrary</u> to popular belief, bats are not blind. Her opinion was <u>contrary</u> to what the others thought.
10	innocuous	(harmless)	***Harmless and unlikely to cause offense*** The comment seemed <u>innocuous</u>, but it hurt his feelings. The puppy's playful barks were <u>innocuous</u> and endearing.
11	convivial	(sociable)	***Cheerful and sociable*** A <u>convivial</u> party was friendly, fun, and lively. The <u>convivial</u> atmosphere made the party enjoyable.
12	jostle	(push)	***To push or bump against someone roughly*** People <u>jostled</u> each other in the crowded market. People <u>jostled</u> to get a better view of the parade.
13	contend	(compete)	***To compete or argue*** Firefighters had to <u>contend</u> with a raging blaze. Teams from different schools will <u>contend</u> in the football tournament.
14	antagonize	(provoke)	***To provoke or annoy someone*** Don't <u>antagonize</u> the dog; it might bite you. Trying to <u>antagonize</u> others is not a good way to make friends.
15	exuberance	(enthusiasm)	***Full of energy, excitement, and cheerfulness*** Her <u>exuberance</u> was contagious, spreading joy to everyone around her. The children's <u>exuberance</u> was evident as they played in the park.

11+ Vocabulary

Once strong and vibrant, full of bloom,
Now strength declines, I meet my doom.
My colours fade, my form grows weak,
A slow decay no cure can seek.

Which word am I?

Word	Meaning	Definition and Examples
01 hybrid	(mixture)	***A mix of two different things*** She bought a new <u>hybrid</u> car that runs on gas and electricity. A <u>hybrid</u> car uses both petrol and electric power.
02 elegant	(graceful)	***Stylish and sophisticated*** The ballerina was <u>elegant</u> and graceful in her movements. The ballroom was decorated in an <u>elegant</u> and sophisticated style.
03 reprehensible	(disgraceful)	***Deserving strong disapproval*** The crime was <u>reprehensible</u> and unforgivable. His <u>reprehensible</u> behaviour alienated his friends.
04 collaborate	(cooperate)	***To work together on a project or task*** We'll <u>collaborate</u> on the project and work on it together. Team members need to <u>collaborate</u> for a successful outcome.
05 wither	(fade)	***Become dry and shrivelled ; fade away*** The plant <u>withered</u> and died without water. His confidence <u>withered</u> under her criticism.
06 consolidate	(combine)	***To combine or strengthen*** He <u>consolidated</u> his knowledge by reviewing his notes before the exam. Let's <u>consolidate</u> our efforts to finish the project faster.
07 threshold	(boundary)	***A point of entry or beginning*** She stood on the <u>threshold</u> of the doorway, unsure if she should enter. We are on the <u>threshold</u> of a new era of technology.
08 reprieve	(respite)	***Delay or cancel a punishment*** The prisoner was granted a temporary <u>reprieve</u> from his sentence. The sunny weather offered a <u>reprieve</u> from the rain.
09 embroiled	(involved)	***Involved deeply in an argument or conflict*** She got <u>embroiled</u> in a scandal at school after being caught cheating. The detective became <u>embroiled</u> in a complex case.
10 process	(method)	***A series of steps to achieve something*** Baking a cake follows a step-by-step <u>process</u>. The human body <u>processes</u> food into energy.
11 jovial	(cheerful)	***Cheerful and friendly*** Her <u>jovial</u> personality made everyone smile. The <u>jovial</u> host made the party atmosphere lively and fun.
12 susceptible	(vulnerable)	***Likely to be influenced or harmed*** He was <u>susceptible</u> to catching colds during the winter. She was <u>susceptible</u> to flattery.
13 primarily	(mainly)	***Mainly or chiefly*** The book is <u>primarily</u> aimed at young readers. The fox <u>primarily</u> hunts small mammals for food.
14 retract	(withdraw (a statement))	***Withdraw a statement or promise*** The cat <u>retracted</u> its claws after playing. Turtles can <u>retract</u> their heads into their shells for protection.
15 coherent	(logical)	***Clearly expressed and easy to understand*** She presented a clear and <u>coherent</u> argument. A well-organized essay is <u>coherent</u> and easy to understand.

	Word	Meaning	Definition and Examples
01	conflict	(dispute)	*A disagreement or fight* There was a <u>conflict</u> of opinion in the meeting. Your plans <u>conflict</u> with mine.
02	proceed	(continue)	*To continue doing something* After a short delay, we were able to <u>proceed</u> with the plan The parade <u>proceeded</u> through the streets.
03	countenance	(tolerate) or (Face)	*Facial expression OR approval* He was reluctant to <u>countenance</u> the use of force Tim's <u>countenance</u> turned sad when he dropped his ice cream.
04	belligerent	(aggressive)	*Hostile and aggressive* His increasingly <u>belligerent</u> attitude caused problems. The <u>belligerent</u> dog growled at anyone who approached its territory.
05	cryptic	(Mysterious)	*Mysterious or puzzling* He gave a <u>cryptic</u> smile. The message was written in a <u>cryptic</u> code.
06	hiatus	(break)	*A break or pause in activity* After a brief <u>hiatus</u>, construction resumed. The band announced a <u>hiatus</u> from touring to focus on projects.
07	exception	(odd)	*Something not included in a general rule - a one-off* With one <u>exception</u>, everyone followed the dress code. Everyone must follow the rules; there are no <u>exceptions</u>.
08	affliction	(suffer)	*Something causing pain or suffering* My cousin suffers from a rare <u>affliction</u> that causes him pain. The flu can be a temporary <u>affliction</u> with fever and aches.
09	improvise	(make up)	*To make something up as you go along* When the guitar broke, the singer <u>improvised</u> the rest of the song. The actor had to <u>improvise</u> when a prop malfunctioned on stage.
10	amicable	(friendly)	*Having a friendly and peaceful relationship* They reached an <u>amicable</u> agreement to end the feud. Despite the disagreement, they parted in an <u>amicable</u> way.
11	adjourn	(postpone)	*To stop or postpone a meeting or activity* The school assembly was <u>adjourned</u> early due to a fire drill. Court is <u>adjourned</u> until tomorrow.
12	contrived	(forced or fake)	*Seeming artificial, forced, or unnatural* The ending of the movie felt <u>contrived</u> and unsatisfying. His apology came across as <u>contrived</u> and insincere.
13	consequence	(result)	*The result of an action* The <u>consequence</u> of his actions was severe. Consider the <u>consequence</u> of your choices before making decisions.
14	scenario	(situation)	*A possible sequence of events* Let's imagine a <u>scenario</u> where you win the lottery! They developed a plan for the worst-case <u>scenario</u>.
15	callous	(mean)	*Uncaring about the feelings of others* His <u>callous</u> disregard for others was shocking. His <u>callous</u> remark hurt her feelings.

11+ Vocabulary

My plans are sneaky, twisted with glee,
Tricks up my sleeve for all to see.
With cunning ways and a mischievous grin,
I plot my schemes where light grows thin.

Which word am I?

	Word	Meaning	Definition and Examples
01	ambiguous	(unclear)	*Not clear or having more than one possible meaning* The question was ambiguous; I couldn't tell what it meant. The instructions were ambiguous, causing confusion among the students.
02	repugnant	(repulsive)	*Extremely distasteful or offensive* The smell of rotten food was absolutely repugnant. The offensive language used in the movie was repugnant.
03	eminent	(famous)	*Famous, respected, and distinguished* The eminent scientist had won many awards for her work. The eminent author gave a lecture at the university.
04	heinous	(wicked)	*Extremely wicked or evil* The crime was so heinous it shocked the nation. They were accused of committing heinous acts.
05	exclaim	(cry out)	*Cry out suddenly because of strong emotion* "What a surprise!" she exclaimed. She will exclaim with joy upon receiving the birthday gift.
06	exploit	(misuse)	*To take advantage of someone or something for personal gain* The squirrel learned to exploit the tree's branches to hide from predators. In the game, the hero must exploit the enemy's weakness to win.
07	deference	(respect)	*Showing respect or politeness* He treated the queen with excessive deference. Bowing is a gesture of deference in some cultures.
08	suffice	(enough)	*Be enough or adequate* One apple will suffice as a snack. A simple apology may suffice to mend the strained relationship.
09	brittle	(fragile)	*Easily broken or fragile* The old branches were brittle and snapped easily. Glass ornaments are brittle and can shatter easily.
10	dubious	(suspicious)	*Doubtful or uncertain* The deal seemed dubious, so he didn't invest. The student gave a dubious explanation for missing the assignment.
11	hone	(sharpen)	*Sharpen or make more effective* She honed her cooking skills over the years. Practice will hone your skills in playing the guitar.
12	depict	(show)	*To represent or show in a picture or words* The movie depicts the struggles of the homeless. The painting will depict a beautiful landscape.
13	advocate	(support)	*A person who supports or speaks in favour of something* Mr. Smith is an advocate for kids' safety. Grandma is an advocate for healthy eating.
14	integrity	(honesty)	*Honesty and moral principles* He is a man of great integrity. The structural integrity of the bridge was compromised.
15	surveillance	(monitoring)	*Close observation, especially of a suspected spy or criminal* The shop had security cameras for surveillance. The government is accused of using mass surveillance to track its citizens.

	Word	Meaning	Definition and Examples
01	clemency	(mercy)	*Mercy or forgiveness* The judge decided to show <u>clemency</u> by giving him a lighter sentence. The teacher showed <u>clemency</u> by giving them extra time to finish homework.
02	harsh	(severe)	*Severe, cruel, or unkind* The critic delivered a <u>harsh</u> review of the play. The punishment seemed <u>harsh</u> for such a minor mistake.
03	strenuous	(demanding)	*Requiring great effort or energy* Running a marathon is a very <u>strenuous</u> activity. <u>Strenuous</u> exercise is good for your health.
04	verbose	(wordy)	*Using more words than needed; long-winded* The professor's lectures were very <u>verbose</u> and difficult to follow. The <u>verbose</u> report put everyone to sleep.
05	ominous	(threatening)	*Giving the impression that something bad is going to happen* There was an <u>ominous</u> feeling in the room. The dark clouds in the sky seemed <u>ominous</u> before the storm.
06	subdued	(quiet)	*Unusually quiet; lacking in energy* The lighting in the restaurant created a <u>subdued</u> atmosphere. She was in a <u>subdued</u> mood after the bad news.
07	alienate	(isolate)	*Make someone feel isolated or unwelcome* Don't <u>alienate</u> your customers with bad service. Constant criticism can <u>alienate</u> friends.
08	connoisseur	(expert)	*An expert with great taste, especially in art, food, etc.* The art critic was considered a <u>connoisseur</u>. A wine <u>connoisseur</u> can distinguish between various types and flavours.
09	apprise	(tell)	*Tell or inform someone of something* Please <u>apprise</u> me of the situation as soon as you have an update. He was not <u>apprised</u> of the changes to the schedule.
10	preclude	(prevent)	*To prevent something from happening* His low grades <u>preclude</u> him from getting into that university. Taking precautions can <u>preclude</u> accidents and injuries.
11	preliminary	(initial)	*Happening before a more important event* These are just the <u>preliminary</u> sketches for the building. The <u>preliminary</u> round will determine which teams advance to the finals.
12	buoyant	(cheerful)	*Able to float or cheerful and optimistic* The helium-filled balloon was <u>buoyant</u> and rose above the crowd at the party. The rubber duck was <u>buoyant</u> in the bathtub and didn't sink.
13	dreary	(gloomy)	*Dull, depressing, and boring* The office had a <u>dreary</u>, drab atmosphere. The rainy weather made the day feel <u>dreary</u>.
14	antique	(old)	*Something old and valuable, usually from a past era* That rocking chair is a genuine <u>antique</u> from the 1800s! The family inherited an <u>antique</u> clock from their grandparents.
15	obstinate	(stubborn)	*Stubborn and refusing to change* My little brother can be <u>obstinate</u> and refuses to listen sometimes. The <u>obstinate</u> child insisted on having ice cream for breakfast.

A tranquil mind, my spirit at ease,
No ripples of worry disturb my peace.
With gentle demeanour and untroubled soul,
My heart rests content, a balanced whole.

Which word am I?

Word	Meaning	Definition and Examples
01 cursory	(hasty)	***Done quickly and without much attention to detail*** Mom gave the kitchen a <u>cursory</u> cleaning before guests arrived. The teacher gave the homework a <u>cursory</u> check.
02 mediocre	(average)	***Average or unremarkable*** I thought the movie was just <u>mediocre</u>, not bad but not amazing either. The food at the restaurant was <u>mediocre</u>.
03 conjecture	(guess)	***A guess based on incomplete information*** His statement is based on <u>conjecture</u>, not facts. Without evidence, the theory remains a <u>conjecture</u> rather than a fact.
04 porous	(leaky)	***Having small holes that allow liquid or air to pass through*** The old, wooden boat was <u>porous</u> and leaked water. Sponge is a <u>porous</u> material that absorbs water easily.
05 revere	(admire)	***To feel deep respect or admiration for something*** Many people <u>revere</u> superheroes because they admire their bravery. Children <u>revere</u> their parents because they love and respect them.
06 displace	(relace)	***To force someone or something out of its usual place*** Earthquakes can sometimes <u>displace</u> large amounts of earth. The floodwaters will <u>displace</u> residents from their homes.
07 conventional	(traditional)	***Following traditional or usual ways*** A <u>conventional</u> breakfast might include cereal with milk. Wearing pyjamas to bed is a <u>conventional</u> bedtime routine for many kids.
08 negate	(nullify)	***To nullify or make ineffective*** The team's loss will <u>negate</u> their chances of winning the tournament. A healthy diet can <u>negate</u> the negative effects of a sedentary lifestyle.
09 placid	(calm)	***Calm and peaceful*** The lake was calm and <u>placid</u>. She had a <u>placid</u> and gentle nature.
10 mogul	(tycoon)	***A very wealthy and powerful businessperson*** The movie <u>mogul</u> was very rich and powerful. The business <u>mogul</u> was known for his successful ventures.
11 indicate	(suggest)	***Point out or suggest something*** The flashing light <u>indicates</u> that the machine is malfunctioning. The sign <u>indicated</u> the direction to the zoo.
12 flagrant	(blatant)	***Openly and shockingly bad or offensive*** Using offensive language is a <u>flagrant</u> disrespect to others. Running in the hallway is a <u>flagrant</u> violation of school rules.
13 emphasis	(importance)	***Special importance given to something*** The teacher put a lot of <u>emphasis</u> on studying hard for the test. The speaker placed <u>emphasis</u> on the importance of teamwork.
14 speculate	(guess)	***Form a theory without firm evidence*** We can only <u>speculate</u> about what happened, as there are no witnesses. They <u>speculated</u> about the cause of the accident.
15 affluent	(wealthy)	***Wealthy or having a lot of resources*** People living in that neighbourhood seem very <u>affluent</u>. The <u>affluent</u> family lived in a big, luxurious house.

	Word	Meaning	Definition and Examples
01	corrosive	(damaging)	***Destructive, able to wear away substances*** Her <u>corrosive</u> criticism destroyed his confidence. The acid had a <u>corrosive</u> effect on the metal.
02	destitute	(poor)	***Extremely poor*** The poor family was <u>destitute</u> and couldn't afford to buy food or clothes. The homeless man was <u>destitute</u> and needed assistance.
03	liable	(responsible)	***Responsible or likely to*** If you break your friend's toy, you're <u>liable</u> to replace it. Parents are liable for their children's well-being.
04	confide	(trust)	***To tell someone a secret, trusting them*** He didn't want to <u>confide</u> his worries to his parents. Friends often <u>confide</u> in each other during difficult times.
05	criterion	(standard)	***A standard by which something is judged*** Admission to grammar school is based on several <u>criteria</u>. One <u>criterion</u> for getting a gold star in class is completing all homework.
06	trawler	(fishing boat)	***A fishing boat that uses a trawl net*** <u>Trawlers</u> can have a negative impact on the ocean by overfishing. The <u>trawler</u> returned to port with a bountiful catch fish.
07	receptive	(open-minded)	***Open and willing to consider something*** The audience was <u>receptive</u> to the comedian's jokes. A good student is always <u>receptive</u> to learning from different sources.
08	permit	(allow)	***To allow or give permission*** My parents won't <u>permit</u> me to stay up past midnight on a school night. The teacher will <u>permit</u> you to leave the classroom when the bell rings.
09	plume	(feather)	***A cloud of smoke etc OR decorative feather or cluster of feathers*** The was a <u>plume</u> of smoke rising from the fire. The peacock displayed its colourful <u>plume</u> of feathers.
10	intermittent	(sporadic)	***Stopping and starting at intervals*** There were <u>intermittent</u> showers throughout the afternoon. The internet <u>connection</u> was intermittent and unreliable.
11	rein	(control)	***A strap for controlling a horse***. The rider pulled on the <u>reins</u> to control the horse. She needs to keep a tight <u>rein</u> on her spending.
12	ambivalence	(uncertainty)	***Having mixed feelings or conflicting emotions*** I feel <u>ambivalence</u> about moving; I'm excited but also sad. Sarah felt <u>ambivalence</u> about joining the soccer team; she loved playing but was nervous about making new friends.
13	defiant	(rebellious)	***Openly refusing to obey*** He maintained a <u>defiant</u> attitude despite the criticism. The student was <u>defiant</u> and refused to follow the rules.
14	complicity	(involvement)	***Involvement in something wrong*** The company denied any <u>complicity</u> in the environmental damage. Accomplices may face charges due to their <u>complicity</u> In the crime.
15	proclaim	(announce)	***To announce officially or publicly*** The town crier <u>proclaimed</u> the new king's announcement. The mayor will <u>proclaim</u> the new city park open during the ceremony.

11+ Vocabulary

With hunger unyielding, my appetite grows,
Consuming all knowledge wherever it flows.
A thirst for discovery, a boundless desire,
My mind ever seeking, a ceaseless fire.

Which word am I?

	Word	Meaning	Definition and Examples
01	obnoxious	(offensive)	***Very unpleasant or offensive*** The <u>obnoxious</u> kid kept interrupting the class with rude comments. The loud and <u>obnoxious</u> music disturbed the neighbours.
02	carve	(cut)	***To cut into a shape*** He <u>carved</u> a beautiful statue out of wood. Artists <u>carve</u> intricate designs into wood or stone.
03	biased	(prejudiced)	***Having a preference or prejudice*** The news article was <u>biased</u> because it only told one side of the story. The judge was <u>biased</u> because he liked one person more than the other.
04	agitated	(disturbed)	***Feeling troubled or disturbed*** The loud thunder made my little brother feel <u>agitated</u>. The noisy crowd <u>agitated</u> the normally calm atmosphere.
05	convenience	(easy)	***Something that makes things easier*** Using a remote control is a great <u>convenience</u> as you don't get up. The microwave is a <u>convenience</u> for quick cooking.
06	voracious	(hungry)	***Having a large appetite; very eager*** My brother has a <u>voracious</u> appetite and always eats huge portions. The <u>voracious</u> reader was always hungry for new stories.
07	reminiscent	(memory)	***Reminding someone of something from the past*** The smell of freshly baked cookies was <u>reminiscent</u> of my old house. The sound of seagulls was <u>reminiscent</u> of our vacation to the beach.
08	fastidious	(meticulous)	***Very careful about details, hard to please*** My aunt is quite <u>fastidious</u> about cleanliness. The chef was <u>fastidious</u> about the quality of ingredients.
09	plummet	(plunge)	***To fall or drop straight down at high speed*** The rock <u>plummeted</u> down the cliffside. The temperature <u>plummeted</u> as winter arrived.
10	rebuke	(reprimand)	***Criticize sharply*** The child got a <u>rebuke</u> from his mother for being rude. The teacher had to <u>rebuke</u> the students for their disruptive conduct.
11	stout	(strong)	***Sturdy and strong; somewhat fat*** The old tree had a <u>stout</u> trunk and wide branches. The <u>stout</u> man struggled to fit into the narrow doorway.
12	crevice	(crack)	***A narrow crack or opening*** They found the missing ring hidden in a <u>crevice</u>. The tiny insect crawled through the <u>crevice</u> in the wall.
13	specimen	(sample)	***An individual example used for study or display*** The scientist carefully examined the insect <u>specimen</u> with a microscope. The biologist collected a <u>specimen</u> of the rare flower for further study.
14	plunge	(dive)	***To jump or fall suddenly*** The temperature took a <u>plunge</u>, dropping suddenly from hot to cold. The brave diver decided to <u>plunge</u> into the deep, dark waters.
15	fallible	(imperfect)	***Capable of making mistakes or being wrong*** Even superheroes in movies are <u>fallible</u> – they mess up sometimes! As a <u>fallible</u> human, I sometimes forget things.

Riddle of the week

With head held high and an arrogant air,
My words proclaim a stature so rare.
Self-importance inflates my every decree,
Blinded by pride, the flaws I can't see.

Which word am I?

	Word	Meaning	Definition and Examples
01	enmity	(hostile)	*A feeling of intense hatred* The siblings had an <u>enmity</u> that lasted for years, always arguing. The long-standing enmity between the two families led to conflict.
02	degenerate	(decline)	*To decline in quality or character* The book's pages had started to <u>degenerate</u> because of age. Pollution can cause the environment to <u>degenerate</u>.
03	erratic	(unpredictable)	*Irregular or unpredictable in movement or behaviour* The patient's breathing pattern became <u>erratic</u>. The car's <u>erratic</u> behaviour indicated a mechanical issue.
04	timid	(shy)	*Lacking in self-assurance or courage; shy* The <u>timid</u> kitten hid under the bed when visitors came over. He was too <u>timid</u> to speak up in the meeting.
05	pompous	(arrogant)	*Arrogant, self-important* The <u>pompous</u> man thought he was better than everyone else. The boss was <u>pompous</u> and always talked about how important he was.
06	conscience	(moral)	*Your inner sense of what's right and wrong* She followed her <u>conscience</u> and did what she believed was right. A guilty <u>conscience</u> may prompt someone to confess their mistakes.
07	imminent	(soon)	*About to happen very soon* With the exams <u>imminent</u>, she felt a sense of dread. The storm clouds indicated that rain was <u>imminent</u>.
08	buffer	(cushion)	*A protective barrier or cushion* The trees served as a <u>buffer</u> against the noise from the highway. The airbags in a car act as a <u>buffer</u> during a collision.
09	ratify	(approve)	*To formally approve or accept* The members of the club met to <u>ratify</u> the decision to hold a bake sale. The students voted to <u>ratify</u> the new school rule about uniforms.
10	reinforce	(strengthen)	*To strengthen or support with additional material* They used steel beams to <u>reinforce</u> the structure of the building. Positive feedback can <u>reinforce</u> good behaviour.
11	busk	(perform)	*Perform music or entertainment in a public place* The musician <u>busked</u> on the street for spare change. He <u>busked</u> on the subway platform, playing his guitar.
12	conspiracy	(plot)	*A secret plan to do something* The friends made a <u>conspiracy</u> to surprise their friend with a party. The students joked about a <u>conspiracy</u> to extend the weekend.
13	feign	(pretend)	*To pretend or fake* She <u>feigned</u> illness to get out of school. He tried to <u>feign</u> surprise when they threw him a surprise party.
14	enthralling	(captivating)	*Fascinating and captivating* The magician's performance was <u>enthralling</u> and left us all speechless. The book was so <u>enthralling</u> that I couldn't put it down.
15	discourse	(discussion)	*Formal discussion or writing on a topic* The teacher gave a <u>discourse</u> to the class about ancient history. The lecture sparked a lively <u>discourse</u> among the students.

A heart devoid of pity or care,
My actions fuelled by a chilling dare.
Remorse and compassion find no place,
Only the goal reflected in my steely gaze.

Which word am I?

	Word	Meaning	Definition and Examples
01	contemplate	(ponder)	***To think deeply about something*** She <u>contemplated</u> her next move carefully in a game of chess. During quiet time, the children <u>contemplate</u> their favourite activities.
02	squalid	(filthy)	***Extremely dirty and unpleasant*** The abandoned house was in <u>squalid</u> condition. The neglected apartment was in <u>squalid</u> condition.
03	vulnerable	(weak)	***Open to attack, harm, or damage*** Elderly people can be especially <u>vulnerable</u> to scams and theft. Baby birds are <u>vulnerable</u> because they can't fly yet.
04	infiltrate	(penetrate)	***To secretly enter or become part of a group*** The explorer had to <u>infiltrate</u> the dense jungle to study the rare plants. The secret agent used a fake ID to <u>infiltrate</u> the criminal organization.
05	ruthless	(merciless)	***Having no pity or compassion*** The evil queen was <u>ruthless</u> in her quest for power. The lion was <u>ruthless</u> when hunting for food.
06	deceptive	(misleading)	***Intending to mislead or trick*** Her <u>deceptive</u> appearance hid her true intentions. The magician used <u>deceptive</u> tricks to amaze the audience.
07	gripe	(complain)	***To complain constantly*** All she did was <u>gripe</u> and complain. It's okay to <u>gripe</u> about a problem, but it's important to find a solution.
08	haggle	(negotiate)	***Negotiate or argue about a price*** They spent a long time <u>haggling</u> over the price. Don't be afraid to <u>haggle</u> when buying a used car.
09	hardy	(strong)	***Able to survive difficult conditions*** He grew up on a farm and was strong and <u>hardy</u>. Some plants are <u>hardy</u> and can survive in extreme temperatures.
10	refute	(disprove)	***Prove something false*** I tried to <u>refute</u> my brother's argument that he should get the last cake. Tim tried to <u>refute</u> the claim that he broke the vase.
11	feral	(wild)	***Wild or untamed, often referring to animals*** He grew up in the wild and had a <u>feral</u> personality. The <u>feral</u> cat lived in the abandoned building.
12	saunter	(stroll)	***Walk in a slow, relaxed manner*** After lunch, we <u>sauntered</u> along the beach. They <u>sauntered</u> through the park, enjoying the sunshine.
13	quell	(suppress)	***To suppress or put an end to something*** The firefighter quickly worked to <u>quell</u> the flames. The police were called to <u>quell</u> the riot and restore order.
14	coerce	(force)	***To force someone to do something*** The kidnappers <u>coerced</u> the victim into revealing their valuables. It's not okay to <u>coerce</u> others into doing things they don't want to do.
15	dogmatic	(opinionated)	***Stubborn, unwilling to listen to others*** He was a <u>dogmatic</u> teacher who refused to consider any other viewpoints. Being <u>dogmatic</u> can hinder open-minded discussions.

A mask I don, a carefully crafted guise,
Concealing the truth that within me lies.
With practiced smiles and words so untrue,
I weave a facade to deceive even you.

Which word am I?

	Word	Meaning	Definition and Examples
01	pretence	(pretend)	***The act of pretending or false appearance*** The whole thing was a <u>pretence</u> to make him look good. His smile was just a <u>pretence</u>; he was actually upset about something.
02	farcical	(absurd)	***Absurd or ridiculous, often in a humorous way*** The whole situation turned into a <u>farcical</u> comedy of errors. The comedy play was full of <u>farcical</u> misunderstandings and mix-ups.
03	putrid	(rotten)	***Rotten, foul-smelling*** The rotten garbage had a <u>putrid</u> smell. He described the movie as a <u>putrid</u> piece of trash.
04	replicate	(duplicate)	***Copy something exactly*** Tim tried to <u>replicate</u> his friend's drawing by copying it. Sarah wanted to <u>replicate</u> her mother's cookies recipe.
05	anecdote	(story)	***A short, amusing, or interesting story*** Grandpa loves telling <u>anecdotes</u> about his childhood adventures. She shared several <u>anecdotes</u> about her time abroad.
06	rueful	(regretful)	***Expressing sorrow or regret in a slightly humorous way*** He gave me a <u>rueful</u> smile after breaking my vase. She gave a <u>rueful</u> shrug when she admitted her mistake.
07	enchanting	(captivating)	***Charming and delightful*** The forest had an <u>enchanting</u> beauty that felt like it was from a fairytale. The <u>enchanting</u> story held the children's attention.
08	celestial	(heavenly)	***Relating to the sky or outer space*** They gazed at the <u>celestial</u> bodies in the night sky. Stars, planets, and the moon are <u>celestial</u> bodies.
09	hygienic	(clean)	***Clean and sanitary*** It's important to maintain good <u>hygienic</u> practices for health. Washing your hands before eating is <u>hygienic</u> as it keeps germs away.
10	diabolical	(awful)	***Extremely wicked or evil*** His <u>diabolical</u> laughter sent shivers down her spine. The villain in the story had a <u>diabolical</u> plan for world domination.
11	deed	(action)	***An action or accomplishment*** Feeding a hungry stray cat is a good <u>deed</u>. Helping others is a good <u>deed</u>.
12	inadvertently	(unintentionally)	***Accidentally, without intending to*** He <u>inadvertently</u> deleted the important document. He <u>inadvertently</u> left his keys at home when rushing to the meeting.
13	figurative	(symbolic)	***Not literal, using metaphor or simile*** The poem used <u>figurative</u> language to create vivid imagery. "Break a leg" is a <u>figurative</u> expression wishing someone good luck.
14	superfluous	(unnecessary)	***Unnecessary; more than enough*** We packed too much, and many of our belongings were <u>superfluous</u>. Bringing an extra umbrella on a sunny day is <u>superfluous</u>.
15	altruistic	(unselfish)	***Unselfishly concerned for the wellbeing of others*** Donating his birthday money to charity was an <u>altruistic</u> act. Her <u>altruistic</u> actions, like volunteering, helped the community.

Riddle of the week

Crumbling walls and shattered dreams remain,
Where neglect and time have left their stain.
A structure once grand, its glory decayed,
A testament to ruin, silently flayed.

Which word am I?

	Word	Meaning	Definition and Examples
01	momentum	(impetus)	**The force or energy that keeps something moving** The protests are gathering momentum. The team gained momentum after scoring the first goal.
02	pliant	(flexible)	**Easily bent or flexible** The gymnast was very pliant, able to do incredible poses. The young tree's branches were pliant in the gentle breeze.
03	impeccable	(flawless)	**Flawless or perfect in every detail** Her work ethic was impeccable. Her performance was impeccable, leaving the audience in awe.
04	incoherent	(confusing)	**Confusing and unclear** After the accident, she was speaking incoherent sentences. When you're tired, your speech may become incoherent.
05	impervious	(resistant)	**Unaffected or unable to be influenced** He seemed impervious to her criticism. The raincoat is impervious to water, so you stay dry even in a storm.
06	compel	(force)	**To force someone to do something** Feeling hungry might compel you to eat a snack. The evidence will compel the jury to reach a verdict.
07	nurture	(care)	**Care for and encourage growth** A good teacher nurtures her students' talents. Parents nurture their children by providing love and support.
08	divulge	(reveal)	**Reveal a secret** Never divulge a secret that a friend told you. Some mysteries are too dangerous to divulge to the public.
09	prelude	(introduction)	**Any action, event, comment, etc. that precedes something else** The short opening act was a prelude to the main concert. The calm before the storm served as a prelude to the fight competition.
10	confound	(confuse)	**To confuse or surprise greatly** The math problem confounded the students as no one could solve it. The magician's trick confounded everyone.
11	hubris	(pride)	**Excessive pride and arrogance** The king's hubris led him defeat in battle. His hubris led to his downfall when he underestimated the opponent.
12	authoritarian	(strict)	**Favouring strict obedience to authority** The authoritarian regime stifled dissent. An authoritarian leader expects complete compliance from the followers.
13	dilapidated	(run-down)	**In very bad condition because of neglect** The city plans to renovate the dilapidated neighbourhood. The old house was dilapidated and needed renovation.
14	pessimist	(cynic)	**Someone who expects the worst outcome** He's a pessimist and always thinks the worst will happen. Don't listen to him, he's just a grumpy pessimist.
15	emphatic	(forceful)	**Expressing something in a strong and forceful way** Her answer was an emphatic no, she definitely did not want to go. The coach gave an emphatic pep talk before the game.

Riddle of the week

With fabrics rich and flavours so bold,
I speak of treasures, stories untold.
Fit for a king, a feast for the eye,
Where luxury whispers, and desires fly.

Which word am I?

	Word	Meaning	Definition and Examples
01	threadbare	(worn-out)	***Thin and worn out due to much use*** His clothes were threadbare and patched. The old carpet was faded and threadbare.
02	bemused	(puzzled)	***Puzzled, confused, or bewildered*** The child's antics left her parents bemused. He looked bemused, because he didn't understand my joke.
03	malign	(slander)	***To speak badly of someone*** Don't malign her just because she's new; she's a nice person. It is unfair to malign others without evidence.
04	pledge	(vow)	***A solemn promise or commitment*** The friends took a pledge never to argue ever again. The students took a pledge to revise hard for the tests.
05	shunt	(move (aside))	***To divert or redirect*** The train was shunted onto a side track. The surgeon created a shunt to bypass the blockage.
06	acrimonious	(angry)	***When people argue in a mean and angry way*** Her acrimonious tone made it clear that she was really angry. Their argument turned acrimonious very quickly after the penalty.
07	quarantine	(isolation)	***Isolate due to disease risk*** The sick dog was placed in quarantine. She was placed in quarantine to protect others from the disease.
08	impromptu	(unplanned)	***Done without planning or preparation*** They gave an impromptu performance for their friends. Her impromptu speech was surprisingly well-received.
09	idle	(inactive)	***Inactive, not doing anything*** Don't sit around idle; there's plenty of work to be done. The machine remained idle until someone started it up.
10	credence	(belief)	***Belief that something is true*** Don't lend credence to baseless gossip. The evidence gave credence to the detective's theory.
11	implicit	(implied)	***Implied but not directly stated*** It's implicit in her message that she won't tolerate further delays. His silence gave implicit permission.
12	demeanour	(behaviour)	***A person's behaviour or manner*** The cat's friendly demeanour made it easy for people to approach him. Her calm and polite demeanour impressed everyone.
13	unkempt	(untidy)	***Having an untidy appearance*** His room was always unkempt, with clothes piled everywhere. The abandoned house had an unkempt garden with overgrown weeds.
14	explicit	(clear)	***Very clear and detailed, leaving no room for doubt*** The contract contained explicit instructions about the procedure. The instructions were explicit, ensuring everyone understood the task.
15	sumptuous	(luxurious)	***Luxurious and expensive*** The Christmas dinner was a sumptuous feast. The royal banquet featured a sumptuous spread of gourmet dishes.

11+ Vocabulary

Though trials may rage and hardships descend,
My spirit remains strong until the very end.
With courage unwavering, a heart true and bold,
I stand as a shield against stories untold.

Which word am I?

	Word	Meaning	Definition and Examples
01	intimidate	(frighten)	***To frighten or threaten someone*** Don't let yourself be <u>intimidated</u> by their tactics. Bullies try to <u>intimidate</u> others with their aggressive behaviour.
02	delve	(explore)	***To search deeply or investigate thoroughly*** Scientists are <u>delving</u> into the mysteries of the brain. He <u>delved</u> into the archives to research his family tree.
03	nostalgia	(longing)	***A sentimental longing for the past*** Looking at old photos gave me a sense of <u>nostalgia</u>. The smell of baking bread always brings a wave of <u>nostalgia</u>.
04	misconceive	(misunderstand)	***To interpret or understand wrongly*** I <u>misconceived</u> what you said, I thought you meant something else. She often <u>misconceived</u> people's intentions.
05	abhorrent	(disgusting)	***Something you strongly dislike***. The living conditions in the camp were <u>abhorrent</u>. The smell from the garbage was <u>abhorrent</u> and unpleasant.
06	whimsical	(playful)	***Playfully quaint, especially in an appealing way*** The <u>whimsical</u> story was full of fairies and talking animals. She had a <u>whimsical</u> sense of humour.
07	collective	(shared)	***Done by a group of people acting together*** The class had a <u>collective</u> effort to clean up the room. The <u>collective</u> effort of the team led to a successful project.
08	encroach	(intrude)	***To go past (exceed) your limit or boundary*** The weeds started to <u>encroach</u> on the flower bed. The construction project should not <u>encroach</u> on protected land.
09	stalwart	(strong)	***Strong, loyal, and reliable*** He was a <u>stalwart</u> defender of his friend, always standing up for him. The <u>stalwart</u> employee had been with the company for two decades.
10	complacent	(smug)	***Satisfied with oneself, maybe too much so*** The team became <u>complacent</u> after years of success. After getting an "A", Tim became <u>complacent</u> and stopped studying.
11	melancholy	(sorrowful)	***A feeling of deep sadness or sorrow*** Listening to slow music always makes me feel a bit <u>melancholy</u>. The rainy weather brought a sense of <u>melancholy</u> to the town.
12	righteous	(moral)	***Morally right or justifiable*** She had a <u>righteous</u> anger toward anyone who bullied others. The <u>righteous</u> leader always stood up for what was fair and just.
13	scour	(search)	***Search or clean or brighten by rubbing hard*** He <u>scoured</u> the house for his missing keys. The maid had to <u>scour</u> the pots to remove the stubborn stains.
14	perish	(die)	***To die or be destroyed*** The old documents will <u>perish</u> if we don't protect them. Without water, the plants will <u>perish</u> in the scorching sun.
15	constraint	(restrict)	***Limitation or restriction*** Budget <u>constraints</u> limited their options. Time <u>constraint</u>: finish your homework in one hour.

Riddle of the week

I may lack a wallet, my pockets are bare,
But finding what's needed, that's my special flair.
From favours to food, with a smile so wide,
I gather my treasures, fuelled by some pride.

Which word am I?

	Word	Meaning	Definition and Examples
01	principle	(belief)	***A fundamental truth or rule*** It's important to stand up for your <u>principles</u>. Honesty is a fundamental <u>principle</u> in building trust.
02	mundane	(ordinary)	***Ordinary, not interesting or exciting*** Most of my chores are pretty <u>mundane</u>, like folding laundry. Doing homework everyday can be <u>mundane</u>.
03	conceit	(vanity)	***Too much pride in oneself*** Out of sheer <u>conceit</u>, he refused the offer of help. His <u>conceit</u> made it challenging for others to work with him.
04	scamper	(run)	***Run with quick light steps*** The squirrel <u>scampered</u> up the tree. The children <u>scampered</u> across the playground.
05	demise	(death)	***The end or death of something*** News of the famous actor's <u>demise</u> spread quickly. The <u>demise</u> of the old building marked progress.
06	artisan	(craftsman)	***A skilled worker who makes things by hand*** The <u>artisan</u> carefully crafted a beautiful wooden table. We hired a skilled <u>artisan</u> to restore our furniture.
07	harness	(control)	***To utilize or control a resource for a specific purpose*** He learned how to <u>harness</u> his anger more effectively. Solar panels <u>harness</u> the power of the sun to generate electricity.
08	guile	(cunning)	***Cunning or deceitful behaviour*** The fox used <u>guile</u> to outsmart the other animals and steal their food. The villain used <u>guile</u> to trick the hero into a trap.
09	scrounge	(beg)	***To try to obtain something without paying for it*** He had to <u>scrounge</u> around for change to buy a snack. They had to <u>scrounge</u> for food after the storm.
10	contrast	(difference)	***To show the difference between things*** The <u>contrast</u> between the two photos was striking. Her outgoing personality was in <u>contrast</u> to his shyness.
11	forestall	(prevent)	***To prevent something by acting in advance*** We need to take action now to <u>forestall</u> any further problems. Installing a security system can help <u>forestall</u> break-ins.
12	obdurate	(stubborn)	***Stubborn and resistant to change*** He was <u>obdurate</u> and refused to change his mind, no matter what. He remained <u>obdurate</u> in the face of all criticism.
13	incision	(cut)	***A cut made with a sharp tool*** The chef made an <u>incision</u> in the fruit to remove the seeds. The surgeon made a small <u>incision</u> to remove the splinter.
14	veteran	(experienced)	***A person who has had long experience in a particular field*** The <u>veteran</u> soldier had many medals from his bravery in battle. She was a <u>veteran</u> surgeon with years of experience.
15	vintage	(old-fashioned)	***High quality and lasting value, or representing the best*** The antique shop had many beautiful <u>vintage</u> items. He had a <u>vintage</u> car collection from the 1930's.

I follow a fight, a pause in the war,
A moment of quiet, and nothing more.
Battles may cease, and tensions subside,
I offer some peace, with nothing to hide.

Which word am I?

	Word	Meaning	Definition and Examples
01	infer	(deduce)	***Deduce or conclude information based on evidence*** We can <u>infer</u> from his silence that he disagrees. Based on the tracks, we can <u>infer</u> that a cat visited our garden.
02	brevity	(brief)	***Briefness or conciseness*** The story's <u>brevity</u> made it easy to read in one sitting. Her reply was admired for its wit and <u>brevity</u>.
03	immense	(enormous)	***Extremely large or vast*** The vastness of the ocean left him feeling a sense of <u>immense</u> awe. The desert stretches for an <u>immense</u> distance, seeming endless.
04	crux	(core)	***The most important or difficult part of something*** Let's get to the <u>crux</u> of the matter and find a solution. Understanding the <u>crux</u> of the problem is essential.
05	truce	(ceasefire)	***A temporary agreement to stop fighting*** The warring countries agreed to a temporary <u>truce</u>. They declared a <u>truce</u> to allow for negotiations.
06	gracious	(kind)	***Kind and polite*** She was a <u>gracious</u> hostess and made everyone feel welcome. The loser accepted defeat with a <u>gracious</u> smile.
07	implicate	(blame)	***To suggest someone is involved in a crime*** The evidence seemed to <u>implicate</u> him in the crime. Don't try to <u>implicate</u> me in your wrongdoing.
08	gibberish	(nonsense)	***Nonsense words*** The baby was babbling in <u>gibberish</u>. His fever caused him to speak in <u>gibberish</u>.
09	aberrant	(abnormal)	***Something that's different or unusual*** The lab results showed an <u>aberrant</u> reading. Her <u>aberrant</u> hairstyle made her stand out in the crowd.
10	asunder	(apart)	***Apart or divided into pieces*** During the earthquake, the old building split <u>asunder</u>. Their relationship was torn <u>asunder</u> by constant fights.
11	petulant	(childish)	***Childishly bad-tempered*** The <u>petulant</u> child threw a tantrum when she didn't get her way. Behave yourself, don't be so <u>petulant</u>!
12	negotiate	(bargain)	***Try to reach an agreement through discussion*** The kids had to <u>negotiate</u> who got to play the video game first. Let's try to <u>negotiate</u> a fair price.
13	slender	(slim)	***Thin and delicate*** The ballerina had long, <u>slender</u> legs. The <u>slender</u> birch trees swayed in the breeze.
14	incentive	(motivation)	***Something that motivates or encourages action*** Mum offered her child a PlayStation as an <u>incentive</u> to pass the exams. The company offered a discount as an <u>incentive</u>.
15	sombre	(gloomy)	***Dark, gloomy or depressing*** The rainy weather created a <u>sombre</u> mood. The funeral had a <u>sombre</u> atmosphere.

Riddle of the week

With angry words, my voice takes flight,
I scold and lash, with all my might.
My harsh critique, a bitter sting,
The weight of blame is what I bring.

Which word am I?

	Word	Meaning	Definition and Examples
01	conviction	(belief)	***A strong belief or a guilty verdict in court*** He spoke with such <u>conviction</u> that everyone believed him. His <u>conviction</u> in justice motivated him to become a lawyer.
02	trudge	(walk heavily)	***Walk slowly with heavy steps*** She <u>trudged</u> home wearily through the snow. The hikers had to <u>trudge</u> through the thick mud during the rainy trek.
03	fumble	(blunder)	***To handle something clumsily*** He <u>fumbled</u> with his keys and dropped them. Don't <u>fumble</u> this opportunity, take your chance!
04	sacred	(holy)	***Holy; deserving of respect*** The old oak tree is <u>sacred</u> to this community. The ancient temple was considered a <u>sacred</u> place of worship.
05	dictate	(command)	***To give orders or command*** He tried to <u>dictate</u> what I should wear. The coach will <u>dictate</u> the team's strategy for the game.
06	pervasive	(widespread)	***Spreading widely*** The smell of smoke was <u>pervasive</u> throughout the house. A <u>pervasive</u> sense of unease filled the room.
07	curb	(control)	***To control or limit something*** We need to <u>curb</u> our spending. Please <u>curb</u> your excitement during the presentation.
08	remnant	(leftover)	***A small remaining piece of something*** Only a tiny <u>remnant</u> of the ancient city wall still stands. The tailor used the <u>remnant</u> of fabric to create a small accessory.
09	preside	(lead)	***Be in charge of a meeting or formal event*** The judge will <u>preside</u> over the trial. The chairman <u>presided</u> over the meeting.
10	pacify	(calm)	***Calm someone who is angry or upset*** She tried to <u>pacify</u> the crying baby with a bottle. They sent in troops to <u>pacify</u> the rioters.
11	incidental	(accidental)	***Happening as a minor part or result of something else*** The damage to the car was purely <u>incidental</u>. The broken toy was an <u>incidental</u> discovery while cleaning the room.
12	persistent	(continuous)	***Continuing despite difficulties, not give up*** The <u>persistent</u> salesperson wouldn't leave us alone. The <u>persistent</u> rain caused flooding in some low-lying areas.
13	deplete	(exhaust)	***To use up or reduce in quantity*** Constant stress had <u>depleted</u> her energy reserves. Overfishing can <u>deplete</u> the population of certain fish.
14	besieged	(surrounded)	***Surrounded and under attack*** The celebrity was <u>besieged</u> by fans at the airport. The castle was <u>besieged</u> by the enemy army from all sides.
15	berate	(scold)	***To scold or criticize harshly*** The customer <u>berated</u> the store manager for the poor service. The coach would <u>berate</u> the players for not giving their best effort.

To follow advice, a warning take,
To listen close, for wisdom's sake.
With careful thought, my words you weigh,
A wiser path you find this way.

Which word am I?

Word	Meaning	Definition and Examples
01 **vanquish**	(conquer)	***To defeat thoroughly; overcome*** The knight hoped to vanquish the dragon and save the princess. He vowed to vanquish his fear of heights.
02 **delirious**	(confused)	***In a state of extreme excitement or confusion*** The lost hikers were delirious from dehydration in the desert. After winning the game, the fans were delirious with joy.
03 **empathy**	(understanding)	***The ability to understand others' feelings*** It's important to have empathy for others. Showing empathy helps create strong connections with people.
04 **heed**	(listen)	***To pay attention to or take notice of*** Motorists are advised to heed the traffic signs. They didn't heed my warnings about the storm.
05 **hasten**	(speed up)	***To move or act quickly*** Let's hasten the redecorating so we can move in sooner. He hastened his steps as it started to rain.
06 **correspondence**	(communication)	***Communication through letters or emails*** There's a lot of correspondence on my desk. They maintained a correspondence through handwritten letters.
07 **furthermore**	(additionally)	***In addition to what has already been said*** The new system is more efficient, and furthermore, it's easier to use. I don't like his attitude; furthermore, I don't trust him.
08 **marred**	(damaged)	***Damaged or spoiled*** The beautiful picnic was marred by a sudden rainstorm. The beautiful painting was marred by a small scratch.
09 **recuperation**	(recovery)	***Recovering from illness or hardship*** After surgery, he needed time for recuperation. A good night's sleep aided her recuperation.
10 **devastate**	(ruin)	***Destroy severely or cause great emotional pain*** The news of his betrayal devastated her. The hurricane can devastate entire communities.
11 **inhibit**	(restrain)	***Hinder or restrain something*** Her shyness inhibited her from speaking in front of the group. Fear can inhibit one's ability to take risks.
12 **diffuse**	(spread)	***Spread out over a wide area*** The police managed to diffuse the tense situation. The aroma of fresh flowers will diffuse throughout the room.
13 **consensus**	(agreement)	***General agreement by a group*** Reaching a consensus in the group was challenging. The team reached a consensus on the best strategy for the project.
14 **momentous**	(significant)	***Of great importance or significance*** Starting high school is a momentous occasion. His graduation was a momentous event for the family.
15 **ooze**	(flow)	***To flow slowly in a thick, sticky way*** Sticky slime started to ooze out of the broken container. The mud began to ooze out from the cracks in the ground.

A storm of anger, I seek to abate,
To soothe troubled spirits, a gentler fate.
With kind words and gestures, tensions decrease,
I strive to restore a feeling of peace.

Which word am I?

	Word	Meaning	Definition and Examples
01	sentiment	(feeling)	*A feeling or emotion* Her birthday card expressed sweet sentiments of love. I share your sentiments on that issue.
02	precedent	(example)	*An earlier event or action that is regarded as an example* There is no precedent for this kind of decision. The court's decision set a precedent for future similar cases.
03	rescind	(cancel)	*Revoke or cancel a decision or order* The school had to rescind the new rule after students complained. The government rescinded the new tax law.
04	listlessness	(low energy)	*Lack of energy or interest* After being sick, I felt a sense of listlessness and didn't want to do much. The heatwave led to a general listlessness among the residents.
05	docile	(obedient)	*Quiet, obedient, and easy to control* The patient was docile and cooperative. The docile puppy quickly learned basic commands.
06	commodity	(product)	*A useful product that can be bought and sold* Things that people buy and sell, like food or oil, are commodities. Oil and natural gas are important commodities for many countries.
07	abyss	(Chasm)	*A super deep and dark hole or pit* The diver looked down into the dark abyss of the ocean. Their relationship fell into an abyss of despair.
08	luminary	(celebrity)	*A person who inspires or influences others* The visiting professor was a luminary in her field. The famous scientist was considered a luminary in the field of physics.
09	excess	(surplus)	*More than what's needed or usual* The store had an excess of winter coats, so they put them on sale. Eating in excess can lead to health problems.
10	placate	(appease)	*To make someone less angry or hostile* The shop offered a discount to placate the unhappy customer. Giving the child a treat sometimes placates her tantrums.
11	steadfast	(loyal)	*Unwavering and determined* He remained steadfast in his beliefs, refusing to change them. She was a steadfast friend, always there in hard times.
12	succinct	(concise)	*Expressed briefly and clearly* Keep your presentation succinct and to the point. The instructions were clear and succinct.
13	imperious	(bossy)	*Arrogant and bossy* His boss had an imperious and demanding manner. His imperious attitude made it challenging for others to work with him.
14	desolate	(sad)	*Empty, barren, and deserted* The landscape after the fire was desolate and barren. The old castle stood desolate on the hill.
15	accountable	(responsible)	*Responsible for what you do* We should all be accountable for our actions. As the leader, she was accountable for the team's success.

11+ Vocabulary

	Word	Meaning	Definition and Examples
01	covet	(desire)	**To desire or wish for something someone else has** Don't <u>covet</u> what others have; focus on your own path. He <u>coveted</u> his neighbour's luxurious sports car.
02	simmer	(boil)	**Stay just below the boiling point** The soup <u>simmered</u> on the stove for an hour. Let tensions <u>simmer</u> down before you try to talk again.
03	procure	(obtain)	**Obtain something, especially with effort** The librarian helped me <u>procure</u> a rare book for my report. The detective needed to <u>procure</u> evidence to solve the case.
04	proximity	(closeness)	**The state of being near** The library is in close <u>proximity</u> to our house so we can walk there. The <u>proximity</u> of the airport was convenient for traveling.
05	designate	(appoint)	**Appoint or choose for a specific role** The area has been <u>designated</u> as a national park. They will <u>designate</u> you as the team captain.
06	exacerbate	(worsen)	**Make a problem worse** The heavy rainfall <u>exacerbated</u> the flooding. Ignoring the issue can <u>exacerbate</u> the problems in the long run.
07	spurn	(reject)	**To reject with disdain or contempt** She <u>spurned</u> his offer of help, wanting to do it independently. He felt <u>spurned</u> after being rejected by the team.
08	pragmatic	(practical)	**Practical and focused on achieving practical results** When problems arise, it's usually best to take a <u>pragmatic</u> approach. Her <u>pragmatic</u> approach made her a great problem-solver.
09	resistance	(opposition)	**The refusal to accept or comply with something** This fabric has good water <u>resistance</u>, perfect for a rain jacket She put up <u>resistance</u> when she found out about changing schools.
10	wince	(flinch)	**Give a slight involuntary grimace in response to pain** I <u>winced</u> in pain when I stubbed my toe. The athlete <u>winced</u> in pain after twisting their ankle during the game.
11	forthright	(honest)	**Direct and honest, sometimes bluntly so** He was praised for his <u>forthright</u> and honest manner. She appreciated his <u>forthright</u> honesty in their discussions.
12	bereft	(deprived)	**Deprived or lacking something** After the fire, he was <u>bereft</u> of all his possessions. The orphan felt <u>bereft</u> of family and love.
13	prestigious	(renowned)	**Inspiring respect and admiration** He went to a <u>prestigious</u> university. Winning the Nobel Prize is a <u>prestigious</u> achievement.
14	ramification	(consequence)	**Consequence of an action** The <u>ramifications</u> of missing the deadline could be serious. The decision to close the factory had serious <u>ramifications</u> for jobs.
15	derelict	(abandoned)	**Abandoned or in a very poor condition** The <u>derelict</u> building is abandoned and falling apart. He was <u>derelict</u> in his duties by leaving the door unlocked.

	Word	Meaning	Definition and Examples
01	transient	(temporary)	*Lasting only for a short time* Many farm workers are <u>transient</u>, moving from place to place. These feelings of sadness are <u>transient</u> and will pass.
02	strive	(work hard)	*To make great efforts to achieve or obtain something* I will <u>strive</u> to get better grades in school. The athlete continued to <u>strive</u> for excellence in every competition.
03	noble	(honourable)	*Having high moral qualities; honourable* It was a <u>noble</u> act to help someone in need. The knight was known for his <u>noble</u> deeds and courage.
04	despicable	(terrible)	*Worthy of hatred or disgust* The news of the crime was truly <u>despicable</u>. Bullying is a <u>despicable</u> behaviour that should not be tolerated.
05	lout	(oaf)	*A rude, badly-behaved person* That <u>lout</u> on the playground was being mean to the smaller kids. The <u>lout</u> disrupted the quiet library with his loud conversation.
06	hitherto	(until now)	*Up to this time or point* <u>Hitherto</u>, she had never travelled outside the country. The documents revealed information <u>hitherto</u> unknown to the public.
07	premise	(assumption)	*A statement that forms the basis for an argument* The whole <u>premise</u> of the movie was a bit ridiculous. It's a false <u>premise</u> that all cats hate water.
08	rift	(gap)	*A crack, split, or break; a serious disagreement* A disagreement caused a <u>rift</u> between the two friends. The earthquake caused a rift in the ground, creating a visible gap.
09	aversion	(dislike)	*A strong dislike or disinclination* He had a strong <u>aversion</u> to spiders. He had an <u>aversion</u> to snakes and avoided them at all costs.
10	gullible	(naïve)	*Easily tricked or deceived* The <u>gullible</u> woman believed the salesman's false claims. Don't be <u>gullible</u>; some offers are too good to be true.
11	stark	(plain)	*Bleak, harsh, or bare in appearance* The difference between night and day was <u>stark</u>. The room was empty with <u>stark</u> white walls.
12	tandem	(together)	*Alongside each other, together* The two projects have to proceed in <u>tandem</u>. The cyclists rode in <u>tandem</u> down the country lane.
13	exposure	(reveal)	*Being subjected to a particular condition or influence* His art gained wide <u>exposure</u> after the gallery show. Prolonged <u>exposure</u> to sunlight can cause skin damage.
14	disparate	(different)	*Completely different and unrelated* The city has areas of extreme wealth and <u>disparate</u> poverty. The group had <u>disparate</u> views on the best solution.
15	covert	(secret)	*Hidden or secretive* The meeting was held in a <u>covert</u> location. The spy operated in <u>covert</u> missions.

I rouse to action, a spark in the night,
With urgency born, I take sudden flight.
Once dull and lethargic, now energy flows,
A force to be reckoned with, as my spirit grows.

Which word am I?

	Word	Meaning	Definition and Examples
01	paradox	(contradiction)	***A statement that seems contradictory but may be true*** The <u>paradox</u> is that the more you have, the more you want. It's a <u>paradox</u> that she feels lonely in a big city.
02	prodigy	(genius)	***A person with exceptional talent, especially a young one*** The chess <u>prodigy</u> could beat people twice her age. She was seen as a child <u>prodigy</u> in mathematics.
03	poultry	(birds)	***Domesticated birds raised for meat and eggs*** For dinner, we ate roast chicken, which is a type of <u>poultry</u>. Chickens and turkeys are common types of <u>poultry</u>.
04	perplexed	(confused)	***Confused or puzzled*** The confusing puzzle left her <u>perplexed</u>. The complex math problem left him <u>perplexed</u> for hours.
05	solidarity	(unity)	***Unity or agreement of feeling*** The workers showed <u>solidarity</u> by going on strike together. Students wore blue shirts to show <u>solidarity</u> with a bullied classmate.
06	interrogate	(question)	***Question someone intensely*** The parents <u>interrogated</u> all the kids to work out who broke the window. The detective will <u>interrogate</u> the suspect to gather information.
07	productive	(efficient)	***Making or creating or achieving a lot*** Staying organized helps me be <u>productive</u> with my homework. Having a well-organized workspace can make you more <u>productive</u>.
08	antipathy	(dislike)	***Strong feeling of dislike*** He felt a strong <u>antipathy</u> towards liver and onions. There was mutual <u>antipathy</u> between the two rival gangs.
09	tyrant	(dictator)	***A cruel and oppressive ruler*** The cruel <u>tyrant</u> ruled the kingdom with an iron fist. The boss was a bit of a <u>tyrant</u>, feared by his staff.
10	augment	(increase)	***To increase or make something larger*** She <u>augmented</u> her English revision by taking extra tuition lessons. New technology can <u>augment</u> our learning abilities.
11	poignant	(touching)	***Evoking a keen sense of sadness or regret*** It was a <u>poignant</u> moment when they said their goodbyes. The movie's <u>poignant</u> ending brought tears to the audience's eyes.
12	analogy	(comparison)	***A comparison between two things to explain something*** Life is an <u>analogy</u> to a journey, with lots of ups and downs. "Life is like riding a bicycle" is a common <u>analogy</u> for maintaining balance.
13	galvanise	(energize)	***Shock or excite into taking action*** The news of the upcoming festival <u>galvanized</u> the whole town. The inspirational speech will <u>galvanize</u> the team to work harder.
14	commute	(travel)	***To travel regularly between home and work*** People who work far away have a long <u>commute</u> to get to work. Some people <u>commute</u> by car, while others use public transportation.
15	preservation	(protect)	***The act of protecting or maintaining something*** The <u>preservation</u> of old buildings is important. <u>Preservation</u> of historical artifacts is crucial for future generations.

	Word	Meaning	Definition and Examples
01	charred	(burnt)	*Burned and blackened* The wood was <u>charred</u> from the fire. The <u>charred</u> remains of the building indicated the severity of the fire.
02	unanimous	(all agreeing)	*Fully in agreement* The vote to have pizza for dinner was <u>unanimous</u> – everyone agreed! The jury reached a <u>unanimous</u> verdict.
03	colloquial	(informal)	*Informal language used in everyday conversation* <u>Colloquial</u> means everyday words, like saying "kid" instead of "child." They used <u>colloquial</u> language and slang in their speech.
04	subterfuge	(deceit)	*Deceit used to achieve a goal* He used <u>subterfuge</u> to trick people into giving him money. The spy used <u>subterfuge</u> to gather information without being detected.
05	shelter	(protection)	*A place that provides protection from weather or danger* We took <u>shelter</u> under a tree when it started raining. Homeless <u>shelters</u> offer a temporary haven for those in need.
06	feasible	(possible)	*Possible, able to be done* Let's see if there's a more <u>feasible</u> way to do this. Developing a <u>feasible</u> plan is crucial for project success.
07	angst	(worry)	*A feeling of deep anxiety or dread* Her breakup caused a lot of <u>angst</u> and sadness. Teenagers often experience <u>angst</u> during their high school years.
08	haughty	(arrogant)	*Arrogant and superior* The <u>haughty</u> princess looked down upon the villagers. His <u>haughty</u> attitude made it challenging to work with him.
09	esteem	(respect)	*Respect and admiration* I hold my former teacher in high <u>esteem</u>. Showing kindness and respect can earn you the <u>esteem</u> of others.
10	conscientious	(careful)	*Doing things carefully, wanting to do what's right* <u>Conscientious</u> people are careful and try their best. A <u>conscientious</u> student completes assignments with attention to detail.
11	catastrophic	(disastrous)	*Involving a sudden and widespread disaster* The flood caused <u>catastrophic</u> damage. The hurricane had a <u>catastrophic</u> impact on the coastal area.
12	plight	(predicament)	*A dangerous or difficult situation* We need to help improve the <u>plight</u> of those living in poverty. The refugees faced a <u>plight</u>, seeking safety and shelter.
13	expedite	(speed up)	*Make something happen faster* We need to <u>expedite</u> the delivery of these supplies. Completing the paperwork in advance will <u>expedite</u> the approval.
14	renounce	(reject)	*Formally give up a right or claim* She <u>renounced</u> her belief in the old ways. The monarch chose to <u>renounce</u> the throne for a simpler life.
15	extreme	(intense)	*Reaching a high or the highest degree* The weather conditions have become <u>extreme</u>. Climbing the mountain requires endurance in <u>extreme</u> conditions.

11+ Vocabulary

Word	Meaning	Definition and Examples
01 prohibit	(forbid)	***To forbid by law or authority, someone more senior*** Smoking is <u>prohibited</u> in many public places. We are <u>prohibited</u> from leaving the school premises on our own.
02 forfeit	(lose)	***To lose or give up something as a penalty*** He had to <u>forfeit</u> the match due to an injury. The team had to <u>forfeit</u> the game due to cheating.
03 beguiled	(charmed)	***Charmed or enchanted; sometimes tricked*** The con artist <u>beguiled</u> her with promises of riches. The magical story <u>beguiled</u> the children, capturing their imagination.
04 procedures	(methods)	***A set of actions or steps to be followed*** It's important to follow the correct safety <u>procedures</u>. Hospitals have strict <u>procedures</u> to ensure patient safety.
05 grimace	(scowl)	***A facial expression of pain or disgust*** He <u>grimaced</u> in pain as the doctor examined his injury. The child made a <u>grimace</u> after tasting the bitter medicine.
06 auspicious	(lucky)	***Favourable or bringing good fortune*** The sunny day was an <u>auspicious</u> start to the wedding. A rainbow is considered an <u>auspicious</u> sign after the rain.
07 seclusion	(isolation)	***The state of being private and away from other people*** The writer sought <u>seclusion</u> in a cabin in the woods. She enjoyed the peace and <u>seclusion</u> of the mountains.
08 scrutinize	(examine)	***To examine or inspect closely and thoroughly*** My parents <u>scrutinized</u> my application form before I submitted them. The detective <u>scrutinized</u> the crime scene for clues.
09 trench	(ditch)	***A long, narrow ditch*** The soldiers dug a <u>trench</u> for protection. Heavy rains caused a <u>trench</u> to form in the field.
10 deluge	(flood)	***A flood, or a large amount of something*** We received a <u>deluge</u> of complaints after the change. The rain turned into a <u>deluge</u>, causing flooding.
11 concur	(agree)	***To agree or have the same opinion*** Sadly, all the experts concur that the situation is only getting worse. The jury had to concur on whether he was innocent or guilty.
12 archive	(records)	***A collection of historical records or documents*** The town's history was stored in a large <u>archive</u> at the library. The museum keeps an <u>archive</u> of ancient manuscripts.
13 bonus	(extra)	***Something given as a reward in addition to what is expected*** The unexpected <u>bonus</u> was a pleasant surprise. Getting extra points on a test can be considered a <u>bonus</u>.
14 privilege	(advantage)	***A special right or advantage*** Many people take the <u>privilege</u> of clean water for granted. It is a <u>privilege</u> to be able to travel the world.
15 intercede	(mediate)	***To intervene or mediate on behalf of others*** The teacher had to <u>intercede</u> when two students began arguing. The UN often tries to <u>intercede</u> in international conflicts.

	Word	Meaning	Definition and Examples
01	nominate	(propose)	***To propose or formally suggest someone for a position*** They <u>nominated</u> him to run for class president. He was <u>nominated</u> for an award for his contribution.
02	imprudent	(reckless)	***Not showing good judgment, unwise*** It was <u>imprudent</u> of him to drive in those stormy conditions. It was <u>imprudent</u> of him to quit his job without a backup.
03	precipitate	(speed up)	***To cause something to happen unexpectedly*** His rash actions <u>precipitated</u> his downfall. A single spark in the dry forest can <u>precipitate</u> a devastating wildfire.
04	deft	(skilful)	***Quick and skilful*** A <u>deft</u> painter has quick and skilful hands. The chef was <u>deft</u> in chopping vegetables.
05	hideous	(ugly)	***Extremely ugly or repulsive*** He wore a <u>hideous</u> mask to the Halloween party. The monster in the movie was portrayed as <u>hideous</u> and terrifying.
06	melee	(brawl)	***A chaotic fight or struggle*** The food fight turned into a crazy <u>melee</u>. The crowded market turned into a <u>melee</u> during the festival.
07	contempt	(disrespect)	***Strong dislike or disrespect*** The student's <u>contempt</u> for the school rules led to frequent detentions. She looked at the mess with <u>contempt</u>.
08	hoarse	(rough)	***Voice sounding rough and harsh, often due to illness*** He woke up with a sore throat and a <u>hoarse</u> voice. After cheering at the game, her voice became <u>hoarse</u>.
09	elusive	(evasive)	***Difficult to find or define*** The thief was <u>elusive</u>, evading capture for months. The answer to the riddle remained <u>elusive</u> for a long time.
10	edifice	(building)	***A large, imposing building*** The old castle was a magnificent <u>edifice</u>. The grand <u>edifice</u> stood tall in the heart of the city.
11	incessant	(continuous)	***Continuing without stopping, often unpleasantly*** The <u>incessant</u> barking of the dog was annoying the neighbours. The <u>incessant</u> rain made it difficult to play outside.
12	simultaneously	(at the same time)	***At the same time*** The twins spoke <u>simultaneously</u>, saying the exact same thing. The dancers moved gracefully, executing their routines <u>simultaneously</u>.
13	notoriety	(infamy)	***Being famous for something bad*** The criminal gained <u>notoriety</u> for his daring escapes. The bank robber gained <u>notoriety</u> for his daring heists.
14	remonstrate	(protest)	***Complain, protest in a forceful manner*** The students remonstrated against the unfair dress code. The citizens gathered to remonstrate against the unjust law.
15	congenial	(friendly)	***Friendly and pleasant*** Our new neighbour is very <u>congenial</u>; she brought us over cookies. The <u>congenial</u> atmosphere at the party made everyone feel welcome.

11+ Vocabulary

Riddle of the week

I make you think, make your anger ignite,
A statement or image that starts up a fight.
I challenge the norm, make boundaries bend,
A spark of unrest, I aim to offend.

Which word am I?

	Word	Meaning	Definition and Examples
01	heralded	(announced)	*Celebrated or announced publicly* The new invention was <u>heralded</u> as a breakthrough. The discovery of the new species was <u>heralded</u> as amazing.
02	transaction	(deal)	*Exchange of goods, services, or funds* I used my credit card for the <u>transaction</u> at the grocery store. I made a <u>transaction</u> with my brother – a teddy for a toy car.
03	altercation	(fight)	*A heated or noisy argument or dispute* The two boys got into an <u>altercation</u> in the hallway. The police were called to break up the <u>altercation</u>.
04	copious	(lots)	*Large in quantity* He drank <u>copious</u> amounts of water before running in the marathon. She took <u>copious</u> notes during the lecture.
05	commemorate	(remember)	*Celebrate the memory of someone or something from the past* We <u>commemorate</u> special days by remembering important events. A statue was erected to <u>commemorate</u> the event.
06	align	(adjust)	*To arrange in a straight line or to support a cause* We had to <u>align</u> the two pieces perfectly to make them fit. The students had to <u>align</u> their chairs in rows for the assembly.
07	provocative	(provoke)	*Intending to cause a reaction, often anger* He kept being <u>provocative</u> by constantly hiding my things. Drawing the graffiti was <u>provocative</u> as so many people hated it.
08	superficial	(shallow)	*shallow or trivial, not significant* Her interest in him was only <u>superficial</u>, based on his looks. The wound was <u>superficial</u> and didn't need stitches.
09	contradiction	(inconsistent)	*Statements or ideas that oppose each other* His excuse was full of <u>contradictions</u>, so the teacher didn't believe him. Saying it's sunny and raining is a <u>contradiction</u>.
10	rugged	(rough)	*Having a rough, irregular, or uneven surface* The <u>rugged</u> coastline was made of sharp rocks. The hikers enjoyed the <u>rugged</u> terrain and challenging trails.
11	compassion	(sympathy)	*Sympathy and desire to help those suffering* She showed <u>compassion</u> towards the less fortunate. Acts of <u>compassion</u> help create a more caring society.
12	succumb	(yield)	*To give in to pressure, temptation, or a negative force* He <u>succumbed</u> to the temptation to eat the entire box of chocolates. She eventually <u>succumbed</u> to the exhaustion and fell asleep.
13	awry	(wrong)	*Off course or not going as planned* Things went <u>awry</u> when their car broke down. The project went awry when they discovered a major error.
14	accustom	(familiar)	*To get used to something over time* I've become <u>accustomed</u> to waking up early for school. It takes time to <u>accustom</u> a new pet to your home.
15	charisma	(charm)	*Personal charm that inspires others* She had a natural <u>charisma</u> that drew people to her. The <u>charismatic</u> leader inspired people with their presence.

	Word	Meaning	Definition and Examples
01	concession	(compromise)	***Something given up, usually in an argument*** Sometimes make the concession of eating a few vegetables. My parents granted me a few concessions to get me to do my chores.
02	aesthetic	(artistic)	***Concerned with beauty and art*** The paintings in the gallery had a very calming aesthetic. Her clothing has a very retro aesthetic – she loves vintage fashion
03	affable	(friendly)	***Friendly and easy to talk to*** My new neighbour seems really affable; he always waves and smiles. I found my new colleagues to be friendly and affable.
04	tendency	(inclination)	***An inclination towards a particular type of thing or action*** I have a tendency to bite my nails when I'm nervous. The child showed a natural tendency for creativity from a young age.
05	adverse	(unfavourable)	***Negative or unfavourable*** The weather conditions were adverse for sailing. The medication might have adverse side effects.
06	spurious	(false)	***False or fake*** The counterfeit money looked real, but it was actually spurious. The police investigated the spurious allegations.
07	exacting	(demanding)	***Requiring a great deal of care, effort, or precision*** The teacher had exacting standards for her students. The job of a surgeon is exacting and demands precision.
08	stagnant	(still)	***Not flowing and often having an unpleasant smell as a result*** My creativity has been stagnant lately. The stagnant pond had become a breeding ground for mosquitoes.
09	resilience	(toughness)	***Ability to recover from difficulties*** Her resilience helped her overcome difficult times. The resilience of the human spirit is inspiring.
10	illiterate	(uneducated)	***Unable to read or write*** Because he never went to school, he is now illiterate. Being illiterate is a significant disadvantage.
11	squander	(waste)	***Waste (money, time, etc.) in a reckless manner*** Don't squander your time playing video games all day. Don't squander this opportunity; make the most of it.
12	translucent	(transparent)	***Semi-transparent*** The stained-glass window was translucent, letting in colourful light. The delicate wings of the butterfly were translucent in the sunlight.
13	glamorous	(attractive)	***Attractive in an exciting and special way*** She dreamed of a glamorous future filled with travel. The movie star looked glamorous on the red carpet.
14	deficiency	(lack)	***A lack of something necessary*** The student's deficiency in math skills was holding her back. A deficiency in vitamins can lead to health problems.
15	respective	(corresponding)	***Belonging or relating separately to each of the things mentioned*** Students returned to their respective classrooms. Each student presented their respective projects during the science fair.

11+ Vocabulary

Though I am young, my mind runs fast,
With knowledge that seems too wise to last.
Adults are surprised by the things I know,
My thoughts and ideas quickly grow.

Which word am I?

	Word	Meaning	Definition and Examples
01	**curtail**	(shorten)	*To reduce or limit* We had to curtail our vacation due to an emergency. They had to curtail their spending to save money.
02	**apportion**	(divide)	*Divide and share out* The teacher apportioned tasks to each group. The chef carefully apportioned the ingredients before mixing the batter.
03	**repercussions**	(consequences)	*Negative unintended consequences of an action* Cheating on the test had serious repercussions. The decision to cut funding had severe repercussions for the local schools.
04	**clasp**	(grip)	*To hold something tightly* She used her hands to clasp the necklace tightly. She wore a beautiful necklace with a silver clasp.
05	**stealth**	(secrecy)	*Cautious or secretive movement* The ninja moved with stealth to avoid being detected. Cats are known for their stealth and agility.
06	**idyllic**	(picturesque)	*Extremely pleasant, peaceful, or picturesque* He dreamt of an idyllic retirement in the countryside. The small village by the lake had an idyllic setting.
07	**assiduous**	(hardworking)	*Hard-working and diligent* His assiduous efforts were finally rewarded with a promotion. An assiduous student studies regularly and does homework on time.
08	**substantial**	(significant)	*Large in amount, size or importance* They received a substantial donation for the charity. A substantial amount of research supports this theory.
09	**scope**	(range)	*The range or size of the area or topic* The scope of the project was too big to finish in one week. This task lies outside the scope of what I am responsible for.
10	**sag**	(droop)	*Sink, droop, or settle from weight or pressure* The old bookshelf started to sag under the weight of too many books. The old sofa began to sag in the middle after years of use.
11	**falter**	(hesitate)	*Hesitate or stumble, lose momentum* His voice started to falter as he became nervous. His confidence began to falter as he faced the challenging task.
12	**precocious**	(advanced)	*Having developed abilities at an earlier age than usual* Her precocious talent in art was recognized early on. The precocious child could read at a level far beyond their peers.
13	**strident**	(loud)	*Harsh, loud, and grating* Her strident voice could be heard over the crowd. The strident sound of the alarm echoed through the building.
14	**amass**	(collect)	*Gather together a large quantity* Squirrels amass a large collection of nuts before winter. Over the years, he amassed a vast fortune.
15	**redundant**	(unnecessary)	*No longer needed or useful* His comments were repetitive and redundant. The extra staff became redundant when the company closed down.

I offer safety, a peaceful space,
A haven from troubles, a sheltered embrace.
Where worries may fade and spirits find rest,
A place of protection, a place truly blessed.

Which word am I?

	Word	Meaning	Definition and Examples
01	frugal	(thrifty)	*Thrifty, careful with money* My grandparents lived a <u>frugal</u> lifestyle. The <u>frugal</u> shopper always looks for discounts and deals.
02	perspire	(sweat)	*To sweat* You tend to <u>perspire</u> a lot when you play sports. After a workout, it's normal to <u>perspire</u> to cool down the body.
03	compile	(collect)	*Put together information from different places* The journalist <u>compiled</u> a report on the corruption scandal. The librarian will <u>compile</u> a list of recommended books for the students.
04	audacious	(bold)	*Bold or daring in a fearless way* The <u>audacious</u> plan seemed impossible, but it just might work. The <u>audacious</u> explorer ventured into uncharted territory.
05	precede	(before)	*To come before in time or order* The storm was <u>preceded</u> by a period of calm weather. The appetizer will <u>precede</u> the main course in the dinner menu.
06	triumph	(victory)	*A great victory or achievement* The team celebrated with cheers after their <u>triumph</u> in the tournament. Their win in the championship was a great <u>triumph</u>.
07	vocation	(profession)	*A person's employment or main occupation* She found her <u>vocation</u> as a nurse and enjoyed helping others. Teaching was her true <u>vocation</u>.
08	sanctuary	(refuge)	*A place of refuge or safety* We found <u>sanctuary</u> from the storm in the mountain cabin. The nature reserve served as a <u>sanctuary</u> for endangered species.
09	garble	(unclear)	*Distort or mix up, making unclear* His message was <u>garbled</u> during transmission. His nervousness caused him to <u>garble</u> his presentation.
10	quagmire	(dilemma)	*A difficult, complex situation OR soft wet area of land* We got stuck in a <u>quagmire</u> of problems that were hard to solve. Walking through the swampy <u>quagmire</u> was a challenging adventure.
11	tirade	(outburst)	*A long angry speech* Dad went on an angry <u>tirade</u> after I broke his favourite mug. Don't let his <u>tirade</u> get to you, he's just stressed.
12	swindle	(deceive)	*Cheat to obtain money fraudulently* The con artist tried to <u>swindle</u> people out of their money. He had a history of <u>swindling</u> people with fake schemes.
13	tedious	(boring)	*Too long, slow, or dull; tiresome or monotonous* Filling out long forms can be a <u>tedious</u> task. The repetitive tasks made the job <u>tedious</u> and uninteresting.
14	burgeon	(flourish)	*To grow or flourish rapidly* The city's population <u>burgeoned</u> in recent years. The flowers began to <u>burgeon</u> in the spring.
15	indiscriminate	(random)	*Done randomly, without careful selection* The wildfire caused <u>indiscriminate</u> destruction. The <u>indiscriminate</u> use of resources can lead to waste.

11+ Vocabulary

I rush along, with danger near,
My warnings fall on a deafened ear.
Careless and hasty, I make my own plight,
Ignoring the signs, with no wisdom in sight.

Which word am I?

	Word	Meaning	Definition and Examples
01	dither	(indecisive)	***To be indecisive or uncertain*** Don't <u>dither</u> about which ice cream flavour to pick, just choose one! She <u>dithered</u> about what to wear, and ended up being late.
02	brusque	(abrupt)	***Blunt or abrupt in speech or manner*** His <u>brusque</u> manner put people off. The manager's <u>brusque</u> response shocked the employees.
03	pinnacle	(summit)	***The highest point or peak of achievement*** Reaching the mountain top was the <u>pinnacle</u> of the hiking trip. Winning the championship was the <u>pinnacle</u> of their sports career.
04	brooding	(moody)	***Deeply thoughtful, often in a moody or gloomy way*** The <u>brooding</u> figure stood alone in the shadows. The <u>brooding</u> character in the movie added a mysterious atmosphere.
05	preposterous	(absurd)	***Absurd, ridiculous*** The idea of flying pigs was <u>preposterous</u>! The idea that the moon is made of cheese is <u>preposterous</u>.
06	avert	(prevent)	***To turn away or prevent*** She <u>averted</u> her eyes from the gruesome scene. The quick action helped <u>avert</u> a potential disaster.
07	reluctant	(hesitant)	***Unwilling and hesitant*** I was <u>reluctant</u> to go to the dentist, but I knew I had to. The <u>reluctant</u> student finally agreed to present the project to the class.
08	conducive	(helpful)	***Helping something to happen, making it easier*** A positive team atmosphere is <u>conducive</u> to productivity. A quiet environment is <u>conducive</u> to focused studying.
09	effervescent	(bubbly)	***Bubbly and lively, like sparkling water*** The children's <u>effervescent</u> energy was infectious. Her <u>effervescent</u> personality brightened up the room.
10	induce	(make happen)	***Persuade, or cause something to happen*** The team tried to <u>induce</u> the opposition into making a mistake. Warm milk may help <u>induce</u> sleep.
11	heedless	(careless)	***Showing a reckless lack of attention*** The children ran <u>heedlessly</u> through the house, making a lot of noise The <u>heedless</u> driver ignored the stop sign and caused an accident.
12	capacity	(ability)	***The maximum amount that something can hold or produce*** He reached his full <u>capacity</u> after weeks of training. The stadium has a seating <u>capacity</u> of 20,000 spectators.
13	chastised	(told off)	***Scolded or criticized severely*** He was <u>chastised</u> for his poor behaviour. The teacher <u>chastised</u> the students for not completing their homework.
14	prominent	(noticeable)	***Important or well-known*** The company's logo was <u>prominently</u> displayed on the building. The <u>prominent</u> mountain peak was visible from miles away.
15	delegate	(reassign)	***To assign tasks or responsibilities to others*** They decided to <u>delegate</u> responsibilities among the team. The manager <u>delegated</u> the task to her assistant.

	Word	Meaning	Definition and Examples
01	flamboyant	(flashy)	*Bold, colourful, and showy* His <u>flamboyant</u> personality always attracted attention. The <u>flamboyant</u> costume stood out in the parade.
02	inept	(incompetent)	*Lacking skill or ability* His <u>inept</u> handling of the situation made things worse. His <u>inept</u> attempts at cooking often ended in disaster.
03	thrifty	(frugal)	*Careful about spending money* My grandma is <u>thrifty</u> and always finds great deals at the store. The <u>thrifty</u> shopper always looks for discounts and buys items on sale.
04	euphoria	(bliss)	*Extreme happiness* I felt a wave of <u>euphoria</u> after crossing the finish line. Winning the <u>championship</u> filled them with euphoria and pride.
05	suppress	(repress)	*Forcibly put an end to* The medicine helps to <u>suppress</u> a cough. She tried to <u>suppress</u> a laugh at the awkward moment.
06	debilitate	(weaken)	*To make someone or something weak* Fear can often <u>debilitate</u> a person's actions. Lack of sleep can <u>debilitate</u> your ability to concentrate.
07	antagonistic	(hostile)	*Showing active opposition or hostility* The bully was always <u>antagonistic</u> toward the smaller kids. The <u>antagonist</u> in the story played a villainous role.
08	invade	(trespass)	*To enter forcefully or intrude* Mosquitoes <u>invaded</u> our campsite at dusk. The reporter's questions <u>invaded</u> my privacy.
09	penchant	(liking)	*A strong liking or preference for something* She has a <u>penchant</u> for wearing brightly coloured clothes. She had a <u>penchant</u> for getting into trouble.
10	bemoan	(regret)	*To express grief or disappointment* He would constantly <u>bemoan</u> his bad luck. The villagers would <u>bemoan</u> the loss of their crops during a bad harvest.
11	exalt	(praise)	*Praise or think very highly of* The victorious team was <u>exalted</u> by their fans. The poet will <u>exalt</u> the beauty of nature in his verses.
12	convoluted	(complicated)	*Complicated and difficult to understand* He lost marks because his answer to the question was <u>convoluted</u>. The plot of the movie was <u>convoluted</u> and hard to follow.
13	construe	(interpret)	*To interpret or understand* <u>Antonym</u>: His intentions were <u>misconstrued</u> by the media. It's easy to <u>construe</u> her smile as a sign of happiness.
14	consistency	(constant)	*Doing something the same way over time* There was a lack of <u>consistency</u> in his performance. The cookie dough should have a smooth <u>consistency</u>.
15	culpable	(blame)	*Deserving blame or responsibility* We are all <u>culpable</u> if we don't protect the environment. The person who caused the accident was deemed <u>culpable</u>.

11+ Vocabulary

With cruelty and harshness, my actions appal,
Uncivilized ways where compassion won't call.
I lack all refinement, both savage and crude,
My behaviour is shocking, uncultured and rude.

Which word am I?

🦉	Word	Meaning	Definition and Examples
01	frenetic	(frantic)	***Fast, energetic, and uncontrolled*** The <u>frenetic</u> pace of the city streets was overwhelming for her. The shoppers were in a <u>frenetic</u> rush as they searched for deals.
02	faux	(fake)	***Artificial or imitation; not genuine***. Her luxurious-looking coat was actually made of <u>faux</u> fur. His <u>faux</u> accent made everyone laugh because it sounded awful.
03	sociable	(friendly)	***Friendly and enjoys being with other people*** My dog is very <u>sociable</u> and loves meeting new people. The <u>sociable</u> child easily made friends at the playground.
04	tentative	(uncertain)	***Unsure or uncertain*** He took a <u>tentative</u> step into the dark, haunted house. We made <u>tentative</u> plans for a vacation next month.
05	petrified	(terrified)	***Extremely frightened*** I'm absolutely <u>petrified</u> of spiders! The loud thunder made the little girl <u>petrified</u> and unable to sleep.
06	conspicuous	(obvious)	***Easily noticeable or standing out*** The police car was <u>conspicuous</u> in the small town. His bright red hat was <u>conspicuous</u> in the crowd.
07	corroborate	(confirm)	***To confirm or support*** The fingerprints <u>corroborated</u> the detective's suspicions. The witness's testimony helped to <u>corroborate</u> the story.
08	captivity	(confinement)	***The state of being imprisoned or confined*** The animals were released from <u>captivity</u>. Animals in <u>captivity</u> may not have the freedom they need.
09	diligent	(hardworking)	***Hard-working and careful*** She was a <u>diligent</u> worker, always focused on her tasks. <u>Diligent</u> students often achieve academic success.
10	barbaric	(brutal)	***Savage or brutal in behaviour*** The <u>barbaric</u> act of violence shocked the world. Some people think fox hunting is cruel and <u>barbaric</u>.
11	quandary	(predicament)	***A dilemma, a difficult choice*** I was in a <u>quandary</u> about whether to go to the party or stay home. Faced with two equally good options, she found herself in a <u>quandary</u>.
12	zenith	(peak)	***The highest point or state*** His career reached its <u>zenith</u> when he turned forty. The sun slowly rose towards its <u>zenith</u>.
13	accolade	(award)	***A special award or praise*** Winning the science fair was a big <u>accolade</u> for Sarah. Winning first place in the race was a big <u>accolade</u>.
14	flattery	(praise)	***Excessive or insincere praise*** She was easily swayed by excessive <u>flattery</u>. She saw through his <u>flattery</u> and knew he was not being genuine.
15	wretched	(miserable)	***Very unhappy or in poor condition*** The lost puppy looked dirty and <u>wretched</u>. She felt <u>wretched</u> after catching the flu.

I belong to the now, the current and new,
Reflecting the times, a fresh point of view.
I might be in fashion, in music, or art,
A style that's modern, a brand-new start.

Which word am I?

#	Word	Meaning	Definition and Examples
01	vindictive	(vengeful)	*Having a strong desire for revenge* His <u>vindictive</u> nature made him seek revenge. Don't be <u>vindictive</u>; try to forgive and move on.
02	contemporary	(modern)	*Modern or current* Her kitchen was very <u>contemporary</u> with all the latest gadgets. The museum had an exhibit on <u>contemporary</u> art with bright colours.
03	sturdy	(robust)	*Strong and robust; able to withstand rough handling* The <u>sturdy</u> table could easily hold a lot of weight. She needed a <u>sturdy</u> pair of boots for the hike.
04	impair	(damage)	*To weaken or damage* His injury <u>impaired</u> his ability to walk. Lack of sleep can <u>impair</u> decision-making.
05	retribution	(punishment)	*Punishment inflicted as vengeance for a wrong* They feared <u>retribution</u> for their actions. Some believe in karma as a form of <u>retribution</u> for one's actions.
06	viable	(workable)	*Capable of working or surviving* This old computer isn't <u>viable</u> anymore. It's too slow and outdated. We need to explore more <u>viable</u> solutions to this problem.
07	indifferent	(unconcerned)	*Having no interest or concern* She seemed <u>indifferent</u> about whether she got the job or not. She seemed <u>indifferent</u> to the outcome of the game.
08	ingenious	(clever)	*Clever and original* He was an <u>ingenious</u> inventor, always creating new gadgets. The student came up with an <u>ingenious</u> solution to the problem.
09	plump	(chubby)	*Rounded, slightly fat* The baby had cute, <u>plump</u> cheeks. The cat looked <u>plump</u> and content after a good meal.
10	camaraderie	(friendship)	*Friendship and trust between people* The shared experience created a sense of <u>camaraderie</u>. The <u>camaraderie</u> among classmates contributed to their success.
11	fictitious	(false)	*Imaginary, not real* The document contained <u>fictitious</u> names and dates. The story was <u>fictitious</u>, filled with magical creatures and adventures.
12	condone	(overlook)	*To accept or allow something even if wrong* The teacher refused to <u>condone</u> the students' bad behaviour. It's not acceptable to <u>condone</u> dishonesty in any situation.
13	comprehensive	(thorough)	*Including all or many details* My teacher gave us a <u>comprehensive</u> study guide for the exam. The report provided a <u>comprehensive</u> overview of the issue.
14	uncouth	(uncivilized)	*Lacking good manners or refinement* It's considered <u>uncouth</u> to chew with your mouth open. The <u>uncouth</u> behaviour of the guest embarrassed everyone at dinner.
15	subside	(lessen)	*Become less intense or violent* The flood waters began to <u>subside</u> after the rain stopped. After the storm, the wind and rain gradually <u>subsided</u>.

With urgency I must be done,
A task delayed will leave you outrun.
My importance cannot be denied,
A command you follow, with focused stride.

Which word am I?

	Word	Meaning	Definition and Examples
01	disparaging	(belittle)	*Saying something to make seem not as good*. The critic wrote a <u>disparaging</u> review of the new play. He made some <u>disparaging</u> remarks about her taste in clothes.
02	perilous	(dangerous)	*Full of danger or risk; hazardous*. The hikers embarked on a <u>perilous</u> journey across the mountain pass. It was a <u>perilous</u> decision to sail the boat directly into the storm.
03	content	(satisfied)	*Satisfied, not wanting more* He seemed <u>content</u> with his simple life. After a good meal, she felt <u>content</u> and happy.
04	competent	(skilled)	*Having the necessary ability or skill* A <u>competent</u> worker does a good job. A <u>competent</u> pilot ensures a safe and smooth flight.
05	deplore	(disapprove)	*To strongly disapprove or regret* Animal lovers <u>deplore</u> any form of cruelty to animals. She <u>deplored</u> the lack of attention to environmental issues.
06	conservation	(protection)	*Protecting and preserving natural resources* Wildlife <u>conservation</u> is essential for the planet. We practice <u>conservation</u> by using less water and recycling.
07	exhort	(urge)	*To strongly encourage or urge someone to do something* The tv commercial <u>exhorts</u> viewers to buy the latest product. Leaders <u>exhorted</u> the citizens to stay united.
08	compensation	(payment)	*Payment to make up for loss or injury* The airline offered financial <u>compensation</u> for the long delay. He received <u>compensation</u> for the injuries at work.
09	imperative	(crucial)	*Absolutely necessary or crucial* Following safety guidelines is <u>imperative</u> on the job site. It is <u>imperative</u> that we act now to address the crisis.
10	beleaguered	(besieged)	*beset (attack from all sides) with hardship and difficulties* The <u>beleaguered</u> manager was facing multiple crises. The castle was <u>beleaguered</u> by enemy forces during the war.
11	exonerate	(innocent)	*Clear someone of blame or guilt* New evidence <u>exonerated</u> him of the crime. The investigation <u>exonerated</u> the company from wrongdoing.
12	replenish	(refill)	*To fill or make complete again* After a long workout, it's important to <u>replenish</u> your fluids. The supermarket staff worked overnight to <u>replenish</u> the shelves.
13	prosperous	(successful)	*Successful and wealthy* They built a <u>prosperous</u> business over many years. The town enjoyed a long period of <u>prosperity</u> because of tourism.
14	animosity	(hostile)	*Strong dislike or hostility* There was a lot of <u>animosity</u> between the two rival teams. She felt no <u>animosity</u> towards him despite their past.
15	fortuitous	(lucky)	*Happening by chance or luck* It was a <u>fortuitous</u> coincidence that they met at the airport. Finding a parking space right in front of the restaurant was <u>fortuitous</u>.

Forms and rules and endless lines,
My process slows, your patience declines.
Red tape tangles, decisions take flight,
I'm a maze of officials, a slow, plodding sight.

Which word am I?

	Word	Meaning	Definition and Examples
01	epiphany	(blank)	*A moment of sudden and great revelation or realization.* While working on the puzzle, she had an <u>epiphany</u> about the solution. The artist's <u>epiphany</u> led to a groundbreaking new style in his work.
02	enigmatic	(mysterious)	*Difficult to understand, mysterious, or puzzling.* The <u>enigmatic</u> symbols carved into stone left archaeologists puzzled. She had an <u>enigmatic</u> smile.
03	reprimand	(scold)	*A formal expression of disapproval* The teacher gave the student a <u>reprimand</u> for talking in class. He received a formal <u>reprimand</u> from his boss for always being late.
04	relapse	(worsen)	*Worsen again after a period of improvement* After getting better, sadly, her illness had a <u>relapse</u>. Skipping medication could lead to a <u>relapse</u> in the patient's condition.
05	apoplectic	(furious)	*Extremely angry or furious* My teacher was <u>apoplectic</u> when he found gum stuck under his desk. The boss was <u>apoplectic</u> after discovering the mistake.
06	substantiate	(verify)	*Provide evidence to support a claim* The evidence helped to <u>substantiate</u> the suspect's guilt. The findings of the study <u>substantiated</u> the theory.
07	segment	(part)	*A portion or part of something* I ate a <u>segment</u> of the orange. The audience was <u>segmented</u> into different age groups.
08	captivating	(enchanting)	*Holding attention in a fascinating way* The speaker was <u>captivating</u> and held the audience's attention. The <u>captivating</u> story kept the audience hooked until the end.
09	reform	(improve)	*Make changes to improve something* We made <u>reforms</u> to the system to improve how it works. After the scandal, the company enacted significant <u>reforms</u>.
10	plausible	(believable)	*Believable or reasonable* It sounded like a <u>plausible</u> excuse, but I wasn't sure if it was true. His explanation sounded <u>plausible</u>, but she still had doubts.
11	bane	(curse)	*Something causing misery or annoyance* Mosquitoes were the <u>bane</u> of our camping trip. Constant interruptions were the <u>bane</u> of his studies.
12	bureaucracy	(administration)	*Many rules and regulations* Navigating the <u>bureaucracy</u> was a slow and frustrating process. <u>Bureaucracy</u> can sometimes slow down decision-making processes.
13	incredulous	(sceptical)	*Unwilling or unable to believe something* He gave her an <u>incredulous</u> look when she told him the news. The students were <u>incredulous</u> when told about the surprise test.
14	turmoil	(confusion)	*A state of great disturbance, confusion, or uncertainty* The whole country is in <u>turmoil</u> after the massive earthquakes. The unexpected news threw her life into <u>turmoil</u>.
15	strategy	(plan)	*A long-term plan of action* The team developed a winning <u>strategy</u> for the championship game. The chess player carefully considered his next <u>strategy</u>.

My heart feels heavy, my spirit is low,
For mistakes I have made, the hurt I bestow.
Regret fills my being, I wish to atone,
With sincere remorse, my wrongdoing I own.

Which word am I?

	Word	Meaning	Definition and Examples
01	**odious**	(hateful)	***Extremely unpleasant or repulsive*** Cleaning the cat's litter box is an <u>odious</u> task. His <u>odious</u> behaviour made him disliked by everyone.
02	**composure**	(calm)	***Staying calm and controlled*** He lost his <u>composure</u> during the heated argument. Maintaining <u>composure</u> during a crisis is crucial for making wise decisions.
03	**benevolent**	(kind)	***Well-meaning and kindly*** The <u>benevolent</u> queen was loved by her people. The <u>benevolent</u> teacher always helped students in need.
04	**forthcoming**	(upcoming)	***Ready to help, or happening soon*** The company was not <u>forthcoming</u> with information about the issue. The author's <u>forthcoming</u> book is highly anticipated by readers.
05	**opulence**	(wealth)	***Wealth and luxury*** The palace was filled with <u>opulence</u>, showing off their wealth. The movie portrayed the <u>opulence</u> of royalty.
06	**ritual**	(ceremony)	***A religious or solemn ceremony; established routine*** Their family had a morning <u>ritual</u> of eating breakfast together. Morning coffee was a cherished daily <u>ritual</u> for her.
07	**patronising**	(condescending)	***Treating others in a condescending way*** His <u>patronising</u> tone of voice made her feel small. Don't be <u>patronising</u> – I know what I'm doing.
08	**contrite**	(sorry)	***Feeling remorse or guilt*** A <u>contrite</u> apology can go a long way in mending fences. After breaking the vase, he was <u>contrite</u> and apologized.
09	**lauded**	(praised)	***Highly praised or celebrated*** The team was <u>lauded</u> for their victory in the tournament. The singer was <u>lauded</u> for her outstanding performance.
10	**withdraw**	(retreat)	***Remove or take away; retreat*** I went to the ATM to <u>withdraw</u> some cash. The soldier had to <u>withdraw</u> from the battle due to injuries.
11	**hoist**	(lift)	***Lift or raise something up, usually with ropes*** The crane <u>hoisted</u> the heavy machinery into place. They will <u>hoist</u> the flag to celebrate the country's independence.
12	**differentiate**	(difference)	***Show the difference between things*** It's difficult to <u>differentiate</u> between the two twins. Teachers help students <u>differentiate</u> between similar-sounding words.
13	**insightful**	(perceptive)	***Showing deep understanding of something*** Her <u>insightful</u> comments added depth to the discussion. The book offered <u>insightful</u> perspectives on the topic.
14	**exempt**	(excused)	***Free from an obligation others must obey*** Children under five are <u>exempt</u> from paying the entrance fee. He was <u>exempt</u> from military service due to a disability.
15	**dissipate**	(fade)	***To gradually disappear or scatter*** The anger in the room slowly <u>dissipated</u> after the talk. The fog will <u>dissipate</u> as the sun rises.

Riddle of the week

I make things shorter, a smaller size,
From lengthy phrases, my power will rise.
I trim and condense with skilful delight,
To save some space, I offer a smaller bite.

Which word am I?

	Word	Meaning	Definition and Examples
01	tantamount	(equivalent)	*Equivalent in seriousness to; virtually the same as* His refusal was <u>tantamount</u> to saying "no". Dropping out of school now is <u>tantamount</u> to ruining your future.
02	implore	(beg)	*To beg desperately* She <u>implored</u> him to reconsider his decision. The child would <u>implore</u> his parents to let him stay up a little longer.
03	disseminate	(spread)	*Spread information widely* The news was <u>disseminated</u> quickly through social media. It's important to <u>disseminate</u> health information widely.
04	demure	(modest)	*Shy, modest* The <u>demure</u> flowers bloomed in shades of pink and white. She gave a <u>demure</u> smile when complimented.
05	presume	(assume)	*To assume, especially without strong evidence* Don't <u>presume</u> to know what I'm thinking. I <u>presume</u> you'll be attending the lesson since it's mandatory.
06	inferno	(fire)	*A large and dangerous fire* This kitchen is so hot, if feels like an <u>inferno</u> in here. The forest fire turned into an <u>inferno</u>, threatening homes.
07	impoverished	(poor)	*Extremely poor* Oliver Twist led an <u>impoverished</u> life as an orphan. The little lost puppy looked <u>impoverished</u>, all skinny and with torn fur.
08	detrimental	(harmful)	*Harmful or damaging* Not getting enough sleep is <u>detrimental</u>. It makes it hard to learn. Smoking is <u>detrimental</u> to your health.
09	unequivocal	(clear)	*leaving no doubt - clear* The evidence against him was <u>unequivocal</u>. A big, happy smile is an <u>unequivocal</u> way to show someone you like them.
10	constitute	(form)	*To be the parts that form something* Twelve months <u>constitute</u> a year. The different colours <u>constitute</u> a beautiful rainbow.
11	ascertain	(find out)	*To find out or make certain* Detectives worked to <u>ascertain</u> the identity of the mysterious thief. The police tried to <u>ascertain</u> the whereabouts of the suspect.
12	tributary	(stream)	*A river or stream flowing into a larger river or lake* The small stream was a <u>tributary</u> of the larger river. Several <u>tributaries</u> feed into the larger lake.
13	torrid	(difficult)	*Very hot and dry; passionate* The <u>torrid</u> summer heat made everyone want to stay indoors. They endured a <u>torrid</u> journey through the desert.
14	concerted	(joint)	*Jointly arranged or planned* We made a <u>concerted</u> effort to finish the project on time. The friends made a <u>concerted</u> effort to organize a surprise party.
15	abbreviate	(shorten)	*To make something shorter or use fewer letters* We can <u>abbreviate</u> 'doctor' as 'Dr.' to save space. Can you <u>abbreviate</u> "laugh out loud" to "LOL" for me?

11+ Vocabulary

Riddle of the week

I stand up tall when danger is near,
A fearless heart, showing no fear.
With noble spirit and a courteous hand,
I protect the weak, as honour is planned.

Which word am I?

	Word	Meaning	Definition and Examples
01	obliterate	(annihilate)	**To destroy completely** The powerful storm obliterated the small house. The explosion seemed to obliterate the old building.
02	counterpart	(equivalent)	**A person or thing similar to another** The boss met with her counterpart at the rival company. The UK detective worked closely with his counterpart in France.
03	imitate	(mimic)	**Copy the behaviour or appearance of someone or something** The child tried to imitate her mother's voice. He was good at imitating the voices of famous actors.
04	profound	(deep)	**Having deep meaning or significance** Her words had a profound impact on the audience. The professor shared a profound quote that left the students thinking.
05	debrief	(review)	**To question or provide information after an event** We'll need to debrief you about the case when you return. After the mission, they had a debrief to discuss what happened.
06	fundamentally	(basically)	**At the most basic level** You need to fundamentally change your attitude. Learning the alphabet is fundamentally important for reading.
07	reiterate	(repeat)	**Repeat to emphasize** I'll reiterate the main points one last time. The teacher had to reiterate the instructions for the assignment.
08	cultivate	(nurture)	**To nurture or develop** He cultivated a reputation as a reliable expert. Farmers cultivate crops to produce food.
09	trait	(characteristic)	**A distinguishing characteristic or quality** Kindness is one of his best personality traits. Creativity and curiosity are valuable personality traits.
10	ferocity	(intense)	**Extreme fierceness or aggressiveness** The lion attacked its prey with ferocity. The storm lashed the coast with unexpected ferocity.
11	gallant	(brave)	**Brave and noble** He received an award for his gallant efforts. The knight was praised for his gallant actions in rescuing the princess.
12	heave	(lift)	**To lift or throw something with great effort** He gave a mighty heave to lift the heavy box. The weightlifter will heave the barbell over his head in one swift motion.
13	depot	(storehouse)	**A storage place for goods or vehicles** The military supplies were stored in a secure depot. The train depot is where the locomotives are kept.
14	drowsy	(sleepy)	**Sleepy** The medication made her feel drowsy. The warm sunlight made her feel drowsy in the afternoon.
15	probe	(investigate)	**To investigate closely** Detectives will probe the crime scene for clues. Scientists use specialized tools to probe the depths of the ocean.

Silly and carefree, I dance and I play,
Ignoring the serious matters of the day.
My concerns are quite shallow, my purpose so slight,
A weightless distraction, a fluffy delight.

Which word am I?

	Word	Meaning	Definition and Examples
01	miscellaneous	(mixed)	*Made up of a variety of unrelated things* There was a miscellaneous box full of random stuff in the attic. The drawer contained a miscellaneous assortment of small items.
02	assuage	(soothe)	*To make something less severe or intense* Mom's hug helped assuage my worries about the test. A warm cup of tea can assuage a sore throat.
03	exemplary	(ideal)	*Serving as an excellent example or model* His work ethic was exemplary. The student received an award for exemplary behaviour.
04	duress	(pressured)	*Threats or pressure forcing someone to do something* He signed the confession under duress. Confessions obtained under duress may not be admissible in court.
05	picturesque	(scenic)	*Visually striking (like a beautiful landscape)* The old, cobblestone village was very picturesque. The village by the river looked picturesque with its colourful houses.
06	cascade	(pass down)	*Series of (quick) things - often with a domino effect* Water cascaded down the waterfall. A cascade of emails flooded her inbox.
07	frivolous	(silly)	*Silly and not serious* She wasted her money on frivolous purchases. Don't waste time on frivolous activities.
08	taxing	(demanding)	*Difficult or demanding* The hike was very taxing and made me extremely tired. The intricate puzzle proved to be a taxing but enjoyable activity.
09	potential	(possible)	*Having the possibility to develop into something* The project has the potential to be very successful. The young artist showed great potential in her paintings.
10	interim	(temporary)	*in between two time points, temporary* They hired an interim manager while searching for a permanent one. The interim leader will manage the team until a new captain is elected.
11	prevail	(win)	*Win or succeed, especially after a struggle* We must prevail against all odds. Good will always prevail over evil in the end.
12	relegate	(demote)	*Demote to a lower position* After making too many fouls, the player was relegated to the bench. Don't relegate me to minor tasks; I have more to offer.
13	vilify	(criticize)	*Speak or write about in an abusively disparaging manner* He was vilified in the news. It's wrong to vilify someone without knowing the truth.
14	debunk	(disprove)	*To prove a claim false* It's important to debunk false information that spreads online. Scientists often debunk myths with evidence.
15	architecture	(design)	*The design and structure of buildings* The architecture of Paris has a very distinct style. The city's architecture includes both modern and historic buildings.

11+ Vocabulary

After a quarrel, when anger takes flight,
I offer kind words to mend and make right.
I seek a solution, a way to agree,
With gestures of peace, hostility to flee.

Which word am I?

🦉	Word	Meaning	Definition and Examples
01	escalate	(intensify)	***To increase rapidly or intensify*** The tension between the two groups <u>escalated</u> quickly. The argument began to <u>escalate</u> into a heated dispute.
02	defame	(slander)	***To damage someone's reputation with false statements*** The rumours were an attempt to <u>defame</u> his reputation. Spreading rumours to <u>defame</u> others is not acceptable.
03	marina	(harbour)	***A harbour for small boats or yachts*** Let's go down to the <u>marina</u> and look at the sailboats. The <u>marina</u> was filled with sailboats enjoying a sunny day.
04	foreboding	(ominous)	***A sense or feeling that something bad will happen*** She had a sense of <u>foreboding</u> about the journey ahead. The dark clouds gave a sense of <u>foreboding</u> before the storm.
05	illusive	(deceptive)	***Deceptive or difficult to find*** His dream of fame proved to be <u>illusive</u>. Finding true happiness can seem <u>illusive</u>.
06	conciliatory	(reconcile)	***Trying to make peace*** We need a <u>conciliatory</u> approach to resolve the dispute. He offered a <u>conciliatory</u> gesture to make amends.
07	archaic	(outdated)	***Very old and outdated*** The old castle had an <u>archaic</u> drawbridge that you had to pull by hand. The language in the ancient book was <u>archaic</u> and hard to understand.
08	clout	(influence)	***Power or influence*** The large corporation has significant economic <u>clout</u>. A celebrity has the <u>clout</u> to impact public opinion.
09	scrooge	(miser)	***A miserly person*** The man was a real <u>scrooge</u> and never donated to charity. Don't be a <u>scrooge</u>! Share some of your candy.
10	prolific	(abundant)	***Producing a lot of something*** The orchard produced a <u>prolific</u> crop of apples. The <u>prolific</u> writer published several books in a single year.
11	hypocritical	(double standards)	***Saying one thing but doing the opposite*** It was <u>hypocritical</u> of her to criticize others when she did the same thing. His <u>hypocritical</u> actions contradicted the values he claimed to uphold.
12	derail	(disrupt)	***Cause something (like a train or conversation) to go off track*** A minor incident <u>derailed</u> the whole project. An obstacle on the tracks can <u>derail</u> a train.
13	crestfallen	(sad)	***Sad and disappointed*** The losing team was <u>crestfallen</u> after the match. She was <u>crestfallen</u> when she didn't get the job.
14	cynic	(doubtful)	***A person who doubts the sincerity of others*** Don't listen to the <u>cynics</u>; believe in yourself. The <u>cynic</u> questioned the motives behind the charity event.
15	lease	(rent)	***To rent or let temporarily*** They signed a <u>lease</u> on the new apartment. The family decided to <u>lease</u> a car for their vacation.

11+ Vocabulary

TEST A

Memory Test

Test A

Write down a 1 word meaning (synonym) for each word.

Refer to the corresponding week for answers (pages 1 to 50)

WK01	Word	Definition
01	futile	
02	mimic	
03	protract	
04	crisis	
05	confer	
06	discernible	
07	fervour	
08	decadent	
09	terrain	
10	hurtle	
11	savoury	
12	constant	
13	postpone	
14	philosophical	
15	nemesis	

WK02	Word	Definition
01	wrath	
02	cathartic	
03	mournful	
04	clamour	
05	unprecedented	
06	compliance	
07	shrewd	
08	slum	
09	flippant	
10	ration	
11	despise	
12	insurmountable	
13	cringe	
14	meander	
15	anguish	

WK03	Word	Definition
01	comrade	
02	stern	
03	ambassador	
04	heritage	
05	coalition	
06	narrative	
07	correlate	
08	detractors	
09	antiquated	
10	predominantly	
11	albeit	
12	indispensable	
13	community	
14	sarcasm	
15	void	

WK04	Word	Definition
01	plethora	
02	fiend	
03	premature	
04	transpire	
05	dearth	
06	diverse	
07	terse	
08	contention	
09	stoic	
10	ardour	
11	vivid	
12	rancid	
13	cordial	
14	immerse	
15	adulation	

Test A

Memory Test

Write down a 1 word meaning (synonym) for each word.

Refer to the corresponding week for answers (pages 1 to 50)

WK05	Word	Meaning
01	delectable	
02	predecessor	
03	incorporate	
04	nuance	
05	perturbed	
06	decree	
07	degrade	
08	ecstatic	
09	duplicity	
10	taint	
11	shove	
12	rudimentary	
13	prudent	
14	lucid	
15	circulate	

WK06	Word	Meaning
01	stampede	
02	pivotal	
03	miserly	
04	pillage	
05	disarray	
06	gregarious	
07	palpable	
08	malevolent	
09	concept	
10	essence	
11	benign	
12	harbour	
13	ravenous	
14	articulate	
15	finesse	

WK07	Word	Meaning
01	scorn	
02	verdict	
03	alleviate	
04	exhibit	
05	surpass	
06	tenacity	
07	congregation	
08	incidence	
09	pedantic	
10	proliferation	
11	gauge	
12	negligent	
13	impartial	
14	rind	
15	arbitrary	

WK08	Word	Meaning
01	chronological	
02	campaign	
03	saturate	
04	supplement	
05	renowned	
06	sceptical	
07	submerge	
08	candour	
09	gung-ho	
10	phenomenon	
11	pitfall	
12	resolution	
13	overwhelming	
14	persona	
15	potent	

Test A

Memory Test

Write down a 1 word meaning (synonym) for each word.

Refer to the corresponding week for answers (pages 1 to 50)

WK09	Word	Meaning
01	enclosure	
02	predicament	
03	emanate	
04	profession	
05	incite	
06	maverick	
07	oblige	
08	curt	
09	residue	
10	disparage	
11	overt	
12	solitude	
13	condemn	
14	spendthrift	
15	sporadic	

WK10	Word	Meaning
01	monotonous	
02	forsake	
03	accumulate	
04	tangible	
05	truant	
06	encompass	
07	certify	
08	precarious	
09	venture	
10	profligate	
11	affinity	
12	annihilated	
13	labyrinth	
14	perpetuate	
15	languish	

WK11	Word	Meaning
01	infuse	
02	readily	
03	strut	
04	compromise	
05	mitigate	
06	attribute	
07	deride	
08	deject	
09	contrary	
10	innocuous	
11	convivial	
12	jostle	
13	contend	
14	antagonize	
15	exuberance	

WK12	Word	Meaning
01	hybrid	
02	elegant	
03	reprehensible	
04	collaborate	
05	wither	
06	consolidate	
07	threshold	
08	reprieve	
09	embroiled	
10	process	
11	jovial	
12	susceptible	
13	primarily	
14	retract	
15	coherent	

Test A

Memory Test
Write down a 1 word meaning (synonym) for each word.

Refer to the corresponding week for answers (pages 1 to 50)

WK13	Word	Meaning
01	conflict	
02	proceed	
03	countenance	
04	belligerent	
05	cryptic	
06	hiatus	
07	exception	
08	affliction	
09	improvise	
10	amicable	
11	adjourn	
12	contrived	
13	consequence	
14	scenario	
15	callous	

WK14	Word	Meaning
01	ambiguous	
02	repugnant	
03	eminent	
04	heinous	
05	exclaim	
06	exploit	
07	deference	
08	suffice	
09	brittle	
10	dubious	
11	hone	
12	depict	
13	advocate	
14	integrity	
15	surveillance	

WK15	Word	Meaning
01	clemency	
02	harsh	
03	strenuous	
04	verbose	
05	ominous	
06	subdued	
07	alienate	
08	connoisseur	
09	apprise	
10	preclude	
11	preliminary	
12	buoyant	
13	dreary	
14	antique	
15	obstinate	

WK16	Word	Meaning
01	cursory	
02	mediocre	
03	conjecture	
04	porous	
05	revere	
06	displace	
07	conventional	
08	negate	
09	placid	
10	mogul	
11	indicate	
12	flagrant	
13	emphasis	
14	speculate	
15	affluent	

11+ Vocabulary

Test A

Write down a 1 word meaning (synonym) for each word.

Refer to the corresponding week for answers (pages 1 to 50)

WK17	Word	Meaning
01	corrosive	
02	destitute	
03	liable	
04	confide	
05	criterion	
06	trawler	
07	receptive	
08	permit	
09	plume	
10	intermittent	
11	rein	
12	ambivalence	
13	defiant	
14	complicity	
15	proclaim	

WK18	Word	Meaning
01	obnoxious	
02	carve	
03	biased	
04	agitated	
05	convenience	
06	voracious	
07	reminiscent	
08	fastidious	
09	plummet	
10	rebuke	
11	stout	
12	crevice	
13	specimen	
14	plunge	
15	fallible	

WK19	Word	Meaning
01	enmity	
02	degenerate	
03	erratic	
04	timid	
05	pompous	
06	conscience	
07	imminent	
08	buffer	
09	ratify	
10	reinforce	
11	busk	
12	conspiracy	
13	feign	
14	enthralling	
15	discourse	

WK20	Word	Meaning
01	contemplate	
02	squalid	
03	vulnerable	
04	infiltrate	
05	ruthless	
06	deceptive	
07	gripe	
08	haggle	
09	hardy	
10	refute	
11	feral	
12	saunter	
13	quell	
14	coerce	
15	dogmatic	

Test A

Write down a 1 word meaning (synonym) for each word.

Refer to the corresponding week for answers (pages 1 to 50)

WK21	Word	Meaning
01	pretence	
02	farcical	
03	putrid	
04	replicate	
05	anecdote	
06	rueful	
07	enchanting	
08	celestial	
09	hygienic	
10	diabolical	
11	deed	
12	inadvertently	
13	figurative	
14	superfluous	
15	altruistic	

WK22	Word	Meaning
01	momentum	
02	pliant	
03	impeccable	
04	incoherent	
05	impervious	
06	compel	
07	nurture	
08	divulge	
09	prelude	
10	confound	
11	hubris	
12	authoritarian	
13	dilapidated	
14	pessimist	
15	emphatic	

WK23	Word	Meaning
01	threadbare	
02	bemused	
03	malign	
04	pledge	
05	shunt	
06	acrimonious	
07	quarantine	
08	impromptu	
09	idle	
10	credence	
11	implicit	
12	demeanour	
13	unkempt	
14	explicit	
15	sumptuous	

WK24	Word	Meaning
01	intimidate	
02	delve	
03	nostalgia	
04	misconceive	
05	abhorrent	
06	whimsical	
07	collective	
08	encroach	
09	stalwart	
10	complacent	
11	melancholy	
12	righteous	
13	scour	
14	perish	
15	constraint	

Test A

WK25	Word	Meaning
01	principle	
02	mundane	
03	conceit	
04	scamper	
05	demise	
06	artisan	
07	harness	
08	guile	
09	scrounge	
10	contrast	
11	forestall	
12	obdurate	
13	incision	
14	veteran	
15	vintage	

WK26	Word	Meaning
01	infer	
02	brevity	
03	immense	
04	crux	
05	truce	
06	gracious	
07	implicate	
08	gibberish	
09	aberrant	
10	asunder	
11	petulant	
12	negotiate	
13	slender	
14	incentive	
15	sombre	

WK27	Word	Meaning
01	conviction	
02	trudge	
03	fumble	
04	sacred	
05	dictate	
06	pervasive	
07	curb	
08	remnant	
09	preside	
10	pacify	
11	incidental	
12	persistent	
13	deplete	
14	besieged	
15	berate	

WK28	Word	Meaning
01	vanquish	
02	delirious	
03	empathy	
04	heed	
05	hasten	
06	correspondence	
07	furthermore	
08	marred	
09	recuperation	
10	devastate	
11	inhibit	
12	diffuse	
13	consensus	
14	momentous	
15	ooze	

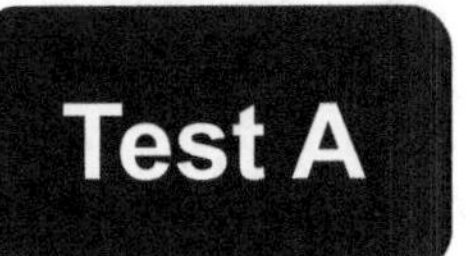

Write down a 1 word meaning (synonym) for each word.

Refer to the corresponding week for answers (pages 1 to 50)

WK29	Word	Meaning
01	sentiment	
02	precedent	
03	rescind	
04	listlessness	
05	docile	
06	commodity	
07	abyss	
08	luminary	
09	excess	
10	placate	
11	steadfast	
12	succinct	
13	imperious	
14	desolate	
15	accountable	

WK30	Word	Meaning
01	covet	
02	simmer	
03	procure	
04	proximity	
05	designate	
06	exacerbate	
07	spurn	
08	pragmatic	
09	resistance	
10	wince	
11	forthright	
12	bereft	
13	prestigious	
14	ramification	
15	derelict	

WK31	Word	Meaning
01	transient	
02	strive	
03	noble	
04	despicable	
05	lout	
06	hitherto	
07	premise	
08	rift	
09	aversion	
10	gullible	
11	stark	
12	tandem	
13	exposure	
14	disparate	
15	covert	

WK32	Word	Meaning
01	paradox	
02	prodigy	
03	poultry	
04	perplexed	
05	solidarity	
06	interrogate	
07	productive	
08	antipathy	
09	tyrant	
10	augment	
11	poignant	
12	analogy	
13	galvanise	
14	commute	
15	preservation	

11+ Vocabulary

Memory Test

Test A

Write down a 1 word meaning (synonym) for each word.

Refer to the corresponding week for answers (pages 1 to 50)

WK33	Word	Meaning
01	charred	
02	unanimous	
03	colloquial	
04	subterfuge	
05	shelter	
06	feasible	
07	angst	
08	haughty	
09	esteem	
10	conscientious	
11	catastrophic	
12	plight	
13	expedite	
14	renounce	
15	extreme	

WK34	Word	Meaning
01	prohibit	
02	forfeit	
03	beguiled	
04	procedures	
05	grimace	
06	auspicious	
07	seclusion	
08	scrutinize	
09	trench	
10	deluge	
11	concur	
12	archive	
13	bonus	
14	privilege	
15	intercede	

WK35	Word	Meaning
01	nominate	
02	imprudent	
03	precipitate	
04	deft	
05	hideous	
06	melee	
07	contempt	
08	hoarse	
09	elusive	
10	edifice	
11	incessant	
12	simultaneously	
13	notoriety	
14	remonstrate	
15	congenial	

WK36	Word	Meaning
01	heralded	
02	transaction	
03	altercation	
04	copious	
05	commemorate	
06	align	
07	provocative	
08	superficial	
09	contradiction	
10	rugged	
11	compassion	
12	succumb	
13	awry	
14	accustom	
15	charisma	

Test A

Memory Test

Write down a 1 word meaning (synonym) for each word.

Refer to the corresponding week for answers (pages 1 to 50)

WK37	Word	Meaning
01	concession	
02	aesthetic	
03	affable	
04	tendency	
05	adverse	
06	spurious	
07	exacting	
08	stagnant	
09	resilience	
10	illiterate	
11	squander	
12	translucent	
13	glamorous	
14	deficiency	
15	respective	

WK38	Word	Meaning
01	curtail	
02	apportion	
03	repercussions	
04	clasp	
05	stealth	
06	idyllic	
07	assiduous	
08	substantial	
09	scope	
10	sag	
11	falter	
12	precocious	
13	strident	
14	amass	
15	redundant	

WK39	Word	Meaning
01	frugal	
02	perspire	
03	compile	
04	audacious	
05	precede	
06	triumph	
07	vocation	
08	sanctuary	
09	garble	
10	quagmire	
11	tirade	
12	swindle	
13	tedious	
14	burgeon	
15	indiscriminate	

WK40	Word	Meaning
01	dither	
02	brusque	
03	pinnacle	
04	brooding	
05	preposterous	
06	avert	
07	reluctant	
08	conducive	
09	effervescent	
10	induce	
11	heedless	
12	capacity	
13	chastised	
14	prominent	
15	delegate	

Memory Test

Test A

Write down a 1 word meaning (synonym) for each word.

Refer to the corresponding week for answers (pages 1 to 50)

WK41	Word	Meaning
01	flamboyant	
02	inept	
03	thrifty	
04	euphoria	
05	suppress	
06	debilitate	
07	antagonistic	
08	invade	
09	penchant	
10	bemoan	
11	exalt	
12	convoluted	
13	construe	
14	consistency	
15	culpable	

WK42	Word	Meaning
01	frenetic	
02	faux	
03	sociable	
04	tentative	
05	petrified	
06	conspicuous	
07	corroborate	
08	captivity	
09	diligent	
10	barbaric	
11	quandary	
12	zenith	
13	accolade	
14	flattery	
15	wretched	

WK43	Word	Meaning
01	vindictive	
02	contemporary	
03	sturdy	
04	impair	
05	retribution	
06	viable	
07	indifferent	
08	ingenious	
09	plump	
10	camaraderie	
11	fictitious	
12	condone	
13	comprehensive	
14	uncouth	
15	subside	

WK44	Word	Meaning
01	disparaging	
02	perilous	
03	content	
04	competent	
05	deplore	
06	conservation	
07	exhort	
08	compensation	
09	imperative	
10	beleaguered	
11	exonerate	
12	replenish	
13	prosperous	
14	animosity	
15	fortuitous	

Memory Test

Write down a 1 word meaning (synonym) for each word.

Refer to the corresponding week for answers (pages 1 to 50)

WK45	Word	Meaning
01	epiphany	
02	enigmatic	
03	reprimand	
04	relapse	
05	apoplectic	
06	substantiate	
07	segment	
08	captivating	
09	reform	
10	plausible	
11	bane	
12	bureaucracy	
13	incredulous	
14	turmoil	
15	strategy	

WK46	Word	Meaning
01	odious	
02	composure	
03	benevolent	
04	forthcoming	
05	opulence	
06	ritual	
07	patronising	
08	contrite	
09	lauded	
10	withdraw	
11	hoist	
12	differentiate	
13	insightful	
14	exempt	
15	dissipate	

WK47	Word	Meaning
01	tantamount	
02	implore	
03	disseminate	
04	demure	
05	presume	
06	inferno	
07	impoverished	
08	detrimental	
09	unequivocal	
10	constitute	
11	ascertain	
12	tributary	
13	torrid	
14	concerted	
15	abbreviate	

WK48	Word	Meaning
01	obliterate	
02	counterpart	
03	imitate	
04	profound	
05	debrief	
06	fundamentally	
07	reiterate	
08	cultivate	
09	trait	
10	ferocity	
11	gallant	
12	heave	
13	depot	
14	drowsy	
15	probe	

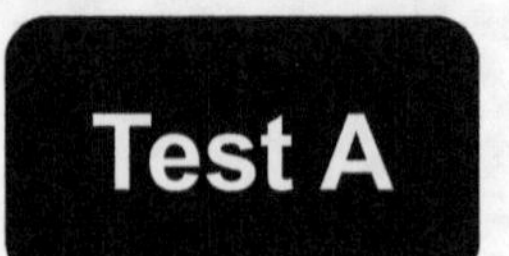

Test A

Write down a 1 word meaning (synonym) for each word.

Refer to the corresponding week for answers (pages 1 to 50)

WK49	Word	Meaning
01	miscellaneous	
02	assuage	
03	exemplary	
04	duress	
05	picturesque	
06	cascade	
07	frivolous	
08	taxing	
09	potential	
10	interim	
11	prevail	
12	relegate	
13	vilify	
14	debunk	
15	architecture	

WK50	Word	Meaning
01	escalate	
02	defame	
03	marina	
04	foreboding	
05	illusive	
06	conciliatory	
07	archaic	
08	clout	
09	scrooge	
10	prolific	
11	hypocritical	
12	derail	
13	crestfallen	
14	cynic	
15	lease	

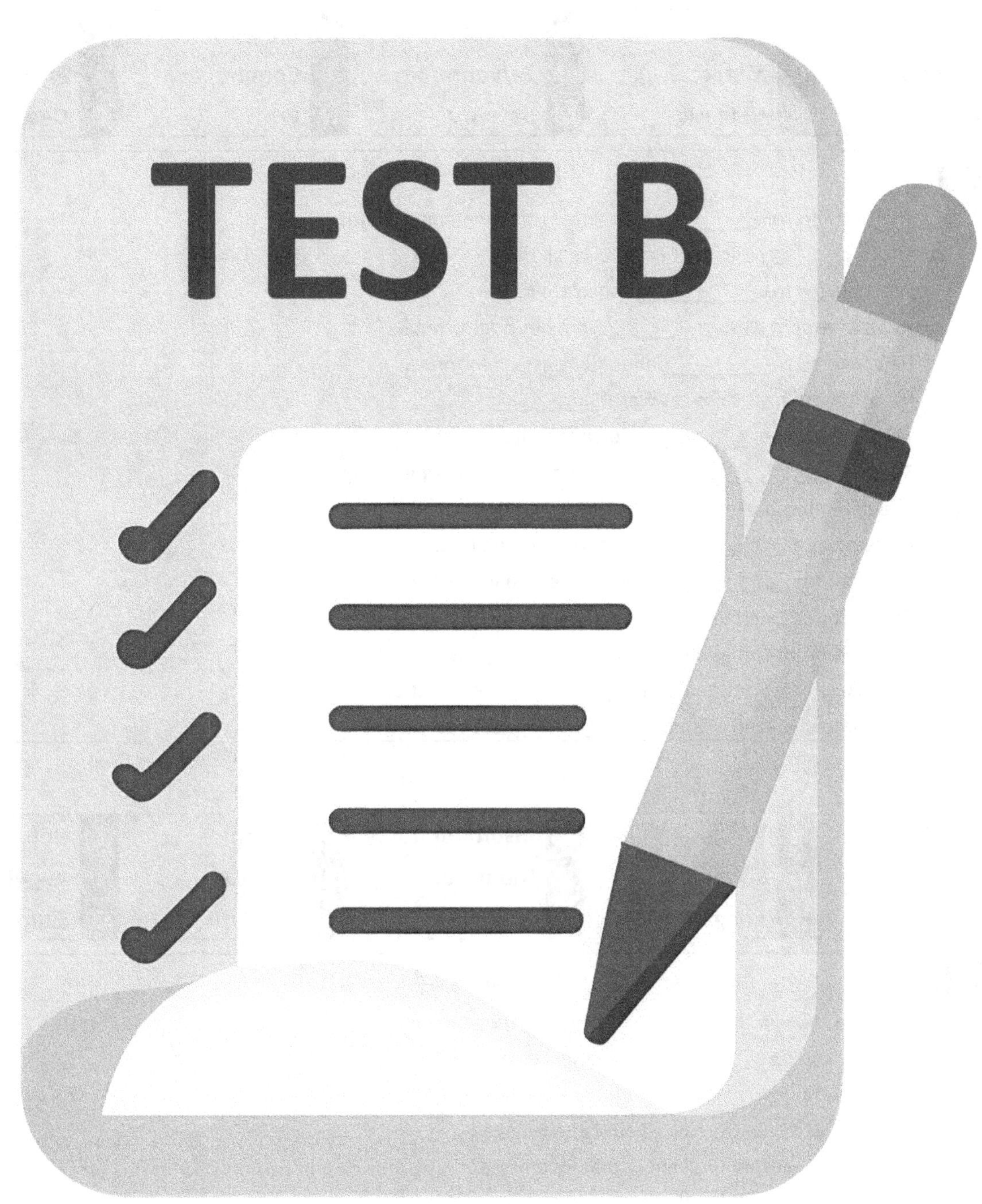
TEST B

A	Hurtle	B	Terrain	C	Constant	D	Philosophical	E	Postpone
F	Discernible	G	Mimic	H	Fervour	I	Confer	J	Protract
K	Futile	L	Nemesis	M	Savoury	N	Crisis	O	Decadent

WK01 — Exercise 1B — Answer

01	The teachers will __________ to discuss the upcoming exams.
02	The __________ rain kept us indoors all day.
03	We indulged in a __________ chocolate dessert.
04	Her excitement was __________ from her bright smile.
05	He spoke with __________ about his passion for music.
06	His efforts to fix the old car were __________.
07	The car began to __________ down the hill.
08	She can __________ the sound of different animals perfectly.
09	The detective finally caught up to his __________.
10	He remained __________ about his recent job loss.
11	They had to __________ the event due to bad weather.
12	The lesson seemed to __________ endlessly.
13	The restaurant serves a variety of __________ dishes.
14	The hikers navigated the rough __________ with caution.
15	The company faced a financial __________ last year.

A	Compliance	B	Wrath	C	Insurmountable	D	Ration	E	Unprecedented
F	Clamour	G	Shrewd	H	Mournful	I	Despise	J	Anguish
K	Flippant	L	Cringe	M	Meander	N	Cathartic	O	Slum

WK02 — Exercise 2B — Answer

01	Her face showed the __________ she felt after the loss.
02	Painting can be a __________ experience for some people.
03	The crowd's __________ could be heard from afar.
04	"When you follow the rules, you are showing __________."
05	I __________ every time I hear that loud noise.
06	He __________d doing chores on the weekend.
07	His __________ remarks did not sit well with the audience.
08	The mountain's steep cliffs seemed __________.
09	The river seemed to __________ through the valley.
10	"She felt __________ when her favourite toy broke."
11	We had to __________ our supplies during the hike.
12	The __________ investor made a wise decision.
13	He grew up in a __________ but worked hard to achieve success.
14	The recent storm was __________ in its intensity.
15	His outburst revealed his deep __________.

A	Detractors	B	Community	C	Heritage	D	Comrade	E	Narrative
F	Predominantly	G	Sarcasm	H	Void	I	Stern	J	Coalition
K	Antiquated	L	Ambassador	M	Albeit	N	Correlate	O	Indispensable

WK03	Exercise 3B	Answer
01	The movie was long, __________ entertaining.	
02	"An __________ is someone who represents their country when visiting others."	
03	The old typewriter was considered __________ by modern standards.	
04	The __________ of organizations worked together on the project.	
05	The local __________ came together to organise a street party.	
06	He treated everyone in the office like a __________.	
07	"When two things happen at the same time, they might __________ with each other."	
08	Despite his __________, he continued his work with dedication.	
09	The castle is part of the nation's __________.	
10	His expertise made him __________ to the team.	
11	The author weaved a compelling __________ in her novel.	
12	The building was __________ painted in blue.	
13	I love getting stuck in traffic," she said with her __________.	
14	Her __________ look made them sit up straight.	
15	He felt a __________ in his life after retiring.	

A	Immerse	B	Dearth	C	Premature	D	Rancid	E	Adulation
F	Fiend	G	Transpire	H	Cordial	I	Vivid	J	Stoic
K	Plethora	L	Terse	M	Ardour	N	Contention	O	Diverse

WK04	Exercise 4B	Answer
01	The actor basked in the __________ of his fans.	
02	She pursued her career with great __________.	
03	The new policy sparked __________ among employees.	
04	They greeted each other with a __________ handshake.	
05	There was a __________ of resources in the area.	
06	The city is known for its __________ culture.	
07	The villain in the story was a true __________.	
08	He liked to __________ himself in a good book.	
09	The market offered a __________ of options.	
10	His decision to quit his job was __________.	
11	The smell of __________ food filled the kitchen.	
12	Despite the pain, she remained __________ and strong.	
13	His __________ reply indicated his impatience.	
14	Let's see what will __________ in the next meeting.	
15	The artist painted with __________ colours and imagination.	

Test B

A	Decree	B	Lucid	C	Delectable	D	Shove	E	Taint
F	Ecstatic	G	Circulate	H	Predecessor	I	Rudimentary	J	Incorporate
K	Prudent	L	Nuance	M	Perturbed	N	Degrade	O	Duplicity

WK05	Exercise 5B	Answer
01	The news began to __________ around the neighbourhood.	
02	The government issued a __________ to ban the activity.	
03	The quality of the product began to __________ over time.	
04	The meal was __________, with each course tasting divine.	
05	His __________ in the deal shocked everyone.	
06	She was __________ when she heard the good news.	
07	We plan to __________ your feedback into the project.	
08	His explanation was clear and __________.	
09	She appreciated the __________ in his argument.	
10	He seemed __________ by the unexpected turn of events.	
11	"A person who came before someone else in a job is called a __________."	
12	It was __________ to save money for unexpected expenses.	
13	The tools they used were quite __________.	
14	He gave the door a __________ to open it.	
15	The scandal threatened to __________ his reputation.	

A	Miserly	B	Essence	C	Disarray	D	Malevolent	E	Benign
F	Gregarious	G	Finesse	H	Harbour	I	Palpable	J	Ravenous
K	Stampede	L	Pillage	M	Pivotal	N	Concept	O	Articulate

WK06	Exercise 6B	Answer
01	He was able to __________ his thoughts clearly.	
02	"The little bump on her skin was __________, which means it wasn't harmful."	
03	She introduced a new __________ for the design.	
04	The room was in __________ after the party.	
05	The __________ of the story lay in its message of hope.	
06	He played the piano with great __________.	
07	She is known for her __________ and friendly nature.	
08	The town was built around a beautiful __________.	
09	The __________ character plotted against the hero.	
10	He was known for his __________ habits.	
11	The tension in the room was __________.	
12	The invaders began to __________ the town.	
13	The __________ moment in the play left the audience in awe.	
14	He felt __________ after the long hike.	
15	The sudden __________ caused panic at the concert.	

A	Pedantic	B	Negligent	C	Rind	D	Proliferation	E	Arbitrary
F	Gauge	G	Tenacity	H	Congregation	I	Surpass	J	Impartial
K	Alleviate	L	Incidence	M	Scorn	N	Verdict	O	Exhibit

WK07	Exercise 7B	Answer
01	The medication helped __________ her pain.	
02	The rules seemed __________ and unfair.	
03	The __________ gathered for the evening service.	
04	The museum will __________ rare artifacts from ancient times.	
05	It was hard to __________ his reaction to the news.	
06	The judge was known for being __________ in his rulings.	
07	The __________ of theft has decreased in recent years.	
08	"If you forget to take care of your pet, that can be __________."	
09	His __________ approach to teaching frustrated the students.	
10	The __________ of weeds made the garden look unkempt.	
11	He peeled the orange and discarded the __________.	
12	She looked at him with __________ when he spoke rudely.	
13	She hopes to __________ her previous record this season.	
14	His __________ helped him finish the marathon.	
15	The jury reached a guilty __________ in the trial.	

A	Phenomenon	B	Chronological	C	Supplement	D	Saturate	E	Submerge
F	Gung-Ho	G	Resolution	H	Overwhelming	I	Sceptical	J	Pitfall
K	Potent	L	Campaign	M	Renowned	N	Persona	O	Candour

WK08	Exercise 8B	Answer
01	The charity launched a __________ to raise awareness.	
02	__________ means telling the truth honestly and clearly.	
03	She arranged the photos in __________ order.	
04	He was __________ about starting his new job.	
05	The response to her book was __________.	
06	His public __________ was very different from his private life.	
07	"A rainbow is a natural __________ that appears after rain."	
08	He learned to avoid the __________ of overworking.	
09	The medicine had a __________ effect on his symptoms.	
10	She is __________ for her stunning art.	
11	His __________ to quit smoking made him feel proud.	
12	The rain began to __________ the ground.	
13	She was __________ of his explanation.	
14	The boat began to __________ after hitting the rock.	
15	He takes a vitamin __________ every day.	

11+ Vocabulary

A	Emanate	B	Solitude	C	Maverick	D	Incite	E	Disparage
F	Sporadic	G	Residue	H	Predicament	I	Profession	J	Oblige
K	Enclosure	L	Condemn	M	Overt	N	Curt	O	Spendthrift

WK09	Exercise 9B	Answer
01	"The teacher will __________ cheating because it isn't fair."	
02	His __________ response took her by surprise.	
03	"It's not nice to __________ someone's work by calling it bad."	
04	A strange smell began to __________ from the kitchen.	
05	The animals were kept safe in an __________ at the zoo.	
06	His speech aimed to __________ change in the community.	
07	He's known as a __________ in the industry.	
08	He felt __________d to help his friend move.	
09	His __________ dislike for the plan was clear.	
10	Teaching is her chosen __________.	
11	There was a __________ left on the plate after washing.	
12	He enjoyed the peace and __________ of the mountains.	
13	Her __________ habits often caused financial problems.	
14	The power outages have been __________ but annoying.	
15	He found himself in a difficult __________.	

A	Tangible	B	Labyrinth	C	Annihilated	D	Affinity	E	Precarious
F	Encompass	G	Perpetuate	H	Certify	I	Languish	J	Accumulate
K	Venture	L	Profligate	M	Forsake	N	Truant	O	Monotonous

WK10	Exercise 10B	Answer
01	She began to __________ savings for her future.	
02	He has a natural __________ for learning languages.	
03	The team was __________ in the final match.	
04	"When someone completes a course, they might receive a certificate to __________ it."	
05	The tour will __________ all the major sights in the city.	
06	She would never __________ her friends in times of need.	
07	The old castle had a __________ of corridors and passages.	
08	The old building continued to __________ in disrepair.	
09	His job became __________ after many years.	
10	The film aimed to __________ positive cultural values.	
11	The ladder was in a __________ position on the roof.	
12	His __________ spending habits worried his family.	
13	The success of the project was __________ in the results.	
14	The student was often __________ from school.	
15	She plans to __________ into a new business field.	

A	Contend	B	Deject	C	Jostle	D	Antagonize	E	Convivial
F	Infuse	G	Contrary	H	Compromise	I	Exuberance	J	Attribute
K	Readily	L	Strut	M	Innocuous	N	Mitigate	O	Deride

WK11	Exercise 11B	Answer
01	His comments seemed to __________ his colleagues.	
02	She could __________ her success to hard work and dedication.	
03	They decided to __________ on the final decision.	
04	"In a race, you must __________ with other runners to try to win."	
05	The decision seemed __________ to his previous statements.	
06	The party had a __________ atmosphere with lots of laughter.	
07	The loss of the game left him feeling __________ed.	
08	They began to __________ his ideas as unrealistic.	
09	"The children showed __________ as they ran around the park."	
10	She likes to __________ her cooking with different flavors.	
11	The substance was found to be __________ and safe.	
12	The crowd began to __________ each other to get closerto the band.	
13	"Wearing a helmet can __________ the risk of injury when biking."	
14	She __________ agreed to help him with his project.	
15	He walked down the street with a confident __________.	

A	Primarily	B	Consolidate	C	Wither	D	Threshold	E	Reprehensible
F	Collaborate	G	Reprieve	H	Retract	I	Process	J	Susceptible
K	Hybrid	L	Coherent	M	Elegant	N	Jovial	O	Embroiled

WK12	Exercise 12B	Answer
01	His speech was clear and __________.	
02	The two artists decided to __________ on a new project.	
03	They decided to __________ their resources for efficiency.	
04	Her __________ dress turned many heads at the party.	
05	He found himself __________ in a heated argument.	
06	The car is a __________ model that uses both gas and electric power.	
07	He greeted everyone with a __________ smile.	
08	The show was __________ targeted at a younger audience.	
09	The company has a new __________ for handling orders.	
10	His actions were considered __________ by many.	
11	"The rain gave us a __________ from the heat on a hot day."	
12	She was asked to __________ her previous statement.	
13	The crops were __________ to sudden changes in weather.	
14	She crossed the __________ of her new home with excitement.	
15	The flowers began to __________ in the summer heat.	

A	Cryptic	B	Hiatus	C	Belligerent	D	Countenance	E	Contrived
F	Proceed	G	Conflict	H	Scenario	I	Adjourn	J	Improvise
K	Amicable	L	Affliction	M	Callous	N	Exception	O	Consequence

WK13	Exercise 13B	Answer
01	The meeting will __________ until next week.	
02	His long-term __________ required constant treatment.	
03	They reached an __________ settlement in the dispute.	
04	His __________ attitude often led to arguments.	
05	His __________ remarks hurt her feelings.	
06	The __________ between the two groups escalated quickly.	
07	He understood the __________ of his actions.	
08	The plot of the movie seemed __________ and unrealistic.	
09	"Her __________ showed she was happy with the decision."	
10	She left a __________ message on his voicemail.	
11	We will make an __________ for this particular case.	
12	The band went on a __________ to work on new music.	
13	He had to __________ when the equipment failed.	
14	"Once everyone is ready, we can __________ with the game."	
15	She prepared for every possible __________.	

A	Brittle	B	Deference	C	Hone	D	Depict	E	Exploit
F	Exclaim	G	Ambiguous	H	Surveillance	I	Integrity	J	Dubious
K	Eminent	L	Heinous	M	Advocate	N	Repugnant	O	Suffice

WK14	Exercise 14B	Answer
01	He continues to __________ for environmental protection.	
02	The directions were __________ and unclear.	
03	The old glass vase was __________ and easily broke.	
04	She showed __________ to her elders out of respect.	
05	The artist was able to __________ the scene with great detail.	
06	He was __________ about the legitimacy of the offer.	
07	She is an __________ scientist in her field.	
08	"Wow, look at that!" she __________ed with delight.	
09	The company decided to __________ the new market opportunity.	
10	"Stealing from others is a __________ act that isn't right."	
11	He practiced daily to __________ his guitar skills.	
12	Her __________ made her a trusted team leader.	
13	The idea of cheating was __________ to him.	
14	A light snack will __________ until dinner.	
15	The store uses __________ cameras for security.	

A	Ominous	B	Strenuous	C	Apprise	D	Buoyant	E	Preclude
F	Alienate	G	Preliminary	H	Obstinate	I	Antique	J	Harsh
K	Dreary	L	Verbose	M	Subdued	N	Connoisseur	O	Clemency

WK15	Exercise 15B	Answer
01	His attitude began to __________ his colleagues.	
02	She collected __________ furniture for her home.	
03	Please __________ me of any changes in the schedule.	
04	He remained __________ despite the challenges he faced.	
05	The judge granted __________ to the defendant.	
06	He is a __________ of fine wines.	
07	The weather was __________ and overcast all day.	
08	His __________ criticism made her feel disheartened.	
09	He remained __________ despite clear evidence against him.	
10	Dark clouds gave an __________ warning of a storm.	
11	His injury will __________ him from competing in the race.	
12	These are just __________ results, subject to change.	
13	The hike was long and __________, but worth it.	
14	The lighting was __________ to create a cozy atmosphere.	
15	His __________ explanation confused the audience.	

A	Speculate	B	Mediocre	C	Flagrant	D	Negate	E	Conventional
F	Revere	G	Emphasis	H	Conjecture	I	Indicate	J	Placid
K	Affluent	L	Cursory	M	Displace	N	Mogul	O	Porous

WK16	Exercise 16B	Answer
01	The neighbourhood is known for being very __________.	
02	His statement was based purely on __________.	
03	She prefers the __________ approach to solving problems.	
04	He gave the report a __________ glance before filing it.	
05	The construction project will __________ many residents.	
06	He placed __________ on the importance of teamwork.	
07	The player was ejected for a __________ foul.	
08	The map will __________ where the treasure is buried.	
09	His performance was __________ compared to his friends.	
10	He is a media __________ with a vast empire.	
11	The latest evidence will __________ his earlier statement.	
12	The lake was calm and __________ in the morning light.	
13	The soil was __________, allowing water to drain quickly.	
14	Many people __________ her for her charitable work.	
15	It's too early to __________ on the outcome of the game.	

A	Rein	B	Complicity	C	Plume	D	Confide	E	Liable
F	Receptive	G	Criterion	H	Permit	I	Corrosive	J	Defiant
K	Proclaim	L	Destitute	M	Ambivalence	N	Intermittent	O	Trawler

WK17	Exercise 17B	Answer
01	"He felt ___________ about the situation because he couldn't decide what to do."	
02	The investigation revealed his ___________ in the crime.	
03	She decided to ___________ in her close friend.	
04	The acid was highly ___________ and dangerous to handle.	
05	Meeting the ___________ for the job is essential.	
06	His ___________ behaviour got him into trouble.	
07	The charity helps feed the ___________ in the community.	
08	The rain was ___________ throughout the day.	
09	He's ___________ for any damage caused by his actions.	
10	He was granted a ___________ to build on the land.	
11	A ___________ of smoke rose from the burning building.	
12	She decided to ___________ her intentions publicly.	
13	He was ___________ to her suggestions for improvement.	
14	He tried to ___________ in his excitement during the interview.	
15	The fishermen set out on their ___________ early in the morning.	

A	Reminiscent	B	Agitated	C	Convenience	D	Plummet	E	Rebuke
F	Voracious	G	Fallible	H	Stout	I	Plunge	J	Biased
K	Fastidious	L	Obnoxious	M	Carve	N	Crevice	O	Specimen

WK18	Exercise 18B	Answer
01	She was visibly ___________ by the unexpected delay.	
02	"Being ___________ means favouring one side too much without being fair."	
03	He used a knife to ___________ his name into the wood.	
04	"Having a park near home is a ___________ for playing outside."	
05	The small ___________ in the wall allowed for light to enter.	
06	Everyone makes mistakes; we are all ___________.	
07	His ___________ attention to detail impressed his boss.	
08	His loud and ___________ behaviour bothered everyone.	
09	The temperature began to ___________ as night fell.	
10	She took a deep breath and prepared to ___________ into the pool.	
11	He received a stern ___________ for his careless remarks.	
12	The old photograph was ___________ of his childhood.	
13	The scientist examined the ___________ under a microscope.	
14	"The old tree in the park is tall and ___________."	
15	He had a ___________ appetite and always asked for seconds.	

A	Conscience	B	Erratic	C	Busk	D	Pompous	E	Reinforce
F	Enmity	G	Enthralling	H	Timid	I	Ratify	J	Buffer
K	Discourse	L	Feign	M	Conspiracy	N	Imminent	O	Degenerate

WK19	Exercise 19B	Answer
01	A line of trees acted as a __________ against the strong winds.	
02	He decided to __________ on the street to earn some money.	
03	His __________ troubled him for not telling the truth.	
04	The detective uncovered a complex __________.	
05	His health began to __________ rapidly.	
06	"The students had a friendly __________ about their ideas."	
07	There was clear __________ between the two opposing teams.	
08	The novel's plot was so __________ that she couldn't put it down.	
09	His __________ driving made other drivers nervous.	
10	He tried to __________ interest in the topic but failed.	
11	A storm is __________, so we should seek shelter.	
12	He acted in a __________ manner, thinking he was superior.	
13	"The committee must __________ the decision before it becomes final."	
14	The bridge was __________d to withstand heavy traffic.	
15	She was too __________ to speak up during the meeting.	

A	Saunter	B	Contemplate	C	Refute	D	Vulnerable	E	Deceptive
F	Haggle	G	Coerce	H	Squalid	I	Feral	J	Gripe
K	Infiltrate	L	Ruthless	M	Hardy	N	Dogmatic	O	Quell

WK20	Exercise 20B	Answer
01	He tried to __________ his friend into agreeing with him.	
02	He took a moment to __________ his next move.	
03	The advertisement was __________ in its claims.	
04	His __________ approach left no room for debate.	
05	The __________ cat roamed the neighbourhood at night.	
06	He began to __________ about the poor service he received.	
07	They decided to __________ over the price of the car.	
08	The plants were __________ and able to survive harsh winters.	
09	The spy planned to __________ the enemy base.	
10	The police tried to __________ the unrest in the city.	
11	The evidence helped __________ his previous claims.	
12	His __________ tactics won him many games.	
13	She decided to __________ through the park on a sunny afternoon.	
14	The __________ conditions in the alley were appalling.	
15	The small town felt __________ to the approaching storm.	

A	Hygienic	B	Altruistic	C	Anecdote	D	Rueful	E	Figurative
F	Inadvertently	G	Celestial	H	Putrid	I	Replicate	J	Deed
K	Enchanting	L	Farcical	M	Pretence	N	Superfluous	O	Diabolical

WK21	Exercise 21B	Answer
01	She made an __________ decision to donate her bonus to charity.	
02	He shared an __________ about his trip to Europe.	
03	We admired the __________ stars through the telescope.	
04	His heroic __________ saved the lives of many people.	
05	The villain's __________ plan was finally revealed.	
06	The garden was __________ with its colourful flowers.	
07	The play was a __________ comedy that left everyone laughing.	
08	She used __________ language to describe her journey.	
09	The restaurant maintained a __________ kitchen for food preparation.	
10	He __________ left his phone at home.	
11	His friendliness was a mere __________ to gain trust.	
12	The garbage had a __________ odour that was hard to ignore.	
13	The scientist tried to __________ the experiment with different variables.	
14	He gave her a __________ smile when she scolded him.	
15	His comments were __________ and added little to the discussion.	

A	Impeccable	B	Incoherent	C	Emphatic	D	Divulge	E	Dilapidated
F	Prelude	G	Hubris	H	Impervious	I	Authoritarian	J	Momentum
K	Pliant	L	Pessimist	M	Nurture	N	Confound	O	Compel

WK22	Exercise 22B	Answer
01	The leader's __________ rule was met with resistance.	
02	The evidence will __________ him to testify in court.	
03	The unexpected twist in the story will __________ readers.	
04	The old building was in a __________ state and needed repairs.	
05	She refused to __________ any details about the surprise party.	
06	His tone was __________ as he made his point clear.	
07	His __________ eventually led to his downfall.	
08	She was known for her __________ taste in fashion.	
09	The raincoat was __________ to water.	
10	His speech was __________ due to his nervousness.	
11	The team had built up __________ for the championship game.	
12	She worked to __________ the young plants in her garden.	
13	He is a __________ who always expects the worst.	
14	The __________ branches of the tree swayed in the wind.	
15	"The __________ is the introduction before the main event."	

A	Threadbare	B	Idle	C	Implicit	D	Sumptuous	E	Unkempt
F	Malign	G	Credence	H	Demeanour	I	Quarantine	J	Bemused
K	Shunt	L	Impromptu	M	Explicit	N	Acrimonious	O	Pledge

WK23	Exercise 23B	Answer
01	Their conversation turned __________ when they disagreed.	
02	She was __________ by the strange behaviour of the animals.	
03	His credentials lent __________ to his theory.	
04	His calm __________ helped diffuse the tense situation.	
05	The instructions were __________ and easy to follow.	
06	He spent his day __________, lounging on the couch.	
07	Her nod gave __________ approval to the plan.	
08	They held an __________ meeting to discuss the issue.	
09	His competitors tried to __________ his reputation.	
10	She made a __________ to support the cause.	
11	The town went into __________ during the outbreak.	
12	"The train was __________ to another track because of construction."	
13	They enjoyed a __________ feast for the holiday.	
14	His __________ coat offered little warmth in the cold.	
15	His __________ appearance was a sign of his lack of care.	

A	Delve	B	Whimsical	C	Melancholy	D	Stalwart	E	Righteous
F	Complacent	G	Abhorrent	H	Collective	I	Constraint	J	Intimidate
K	Scour	L	Encroach	M	Misconceive	N	Perish	O	Nostalgia

WK24	Exercise 24B	Answer
01	The crime was considered __________ by the community.	
02	The __________ effort led to the project's success.	
03	"She became __________ and stopped studying because she thought she knew it all."	
04	Time __________ forced them to make a quick decision.	
05	"He loves to __________ into his books and learn new things."	
06	The new construction would __________ on the nature reserve.	
07	His height and stern expression could __________ people.	
08	He felt a sense of __________ after hearing the news.	
09	They __________d his intentions and reacted harshly.	
10	She felt a wave of __________ as she visited her childhood home.	
11	The flowers will __________ if not watered regularly.	
12	His __________ anger over the injustice was justified.	
13	He had to __________ the house to find his missing keys.	
14	She was a __________ supporter of the team's efforts.	
15	Her __________ designs brought joy to the art show.	

A	Veteran	B	Guile	C	Contrast	D	Demise	E	Scamper
F	Mundane	G	Forestall	H	Incision	I	Artisan	J	Vintage
K	Obdurate	L	Harness	M	Conceit	N	Scrounge	O	Principle

WK25	Exercise 25B	Answer
01	He is a skilled __________ known for his handcrafted goods.	
02	His __________ made it hard for him to work with others.	
03	The new painting provided a stark __________ to the older pieces.	
04	The company's __________ was due to poor management.	
05	She tried to __________ their departure by starting a conversation.	
06	"Being honest and straightforward is better than using __________."	
07	She tried to __________ the energy of the team for the project.	
08	The surgeon made a precise __________ during the operation.	
09	His daily routine was __________ and uninspiring.	
10	He remained __________ in his stance despite new evidence.	
11	She stood firm on her __________ of honesty.	
12	The squirrel would __________ up the tree at the sound of a noise.	
13	He tried to __________ up enough money for a meal.	
14	He is a __________ of the armed forces with years of service.	
15	The shop specializes in selling __________ clothing.	

A	Slender	B	Aberrant	C	Negotiate	D	Petulant	E	Implicate
F	Truce	G	Gracious	H	Brevity	I	Infer	J	Asunder
K	Crux	L	Gibberish	M	Sombre	N	Immense	O	Incentive

WK26	Exercise 26B	Answer
01	His __________ behaviour concerned his family.	
02	The bridge was torn __________ by the floodwaters.	
03	His speech was noted for its __________ and clarity.	
04	He quickly got to the __________ of the issue in the meeting.	
05	His response was __________ and made little sense.	
06	She was __________ in accepting her award.	
07	The view from the mountain was __________ and breathtaking.	
08	The evidence seemed to __________ him in the crime.	
09	The bonus was an __________ to increase productivity.	
10	Based on the clues, she could __________ what happened.	
11	They tried to __________ a better deal for the contract.	
12	His __________ attitude made it hard to work with him.	
13	"The young tree is still __________ and needs time to grow."	
14	The mood was __________ after hearing the bad news.	
15	The two parties agreed to a temporary __________.	

A	Preside	B	Incidental	C	Remnant	D	Sacred	E	Besieged
F	Fumble	G	Deplete	H	Dictate	I	Conviction	J	Curb
K	Pervasive	L	Berate	M	Trudge	N	Pacify	O	Persistent

WK27	Exercise 27B	Answer
01	He began to __________ his team for their poor performance.	
02	The castle was __________ by enemy forces for weeks.	
03	His __________ in his beliefs was admirable.	
04	She tried to __________ her desire for junk food.	
05	Overfishing can __________ the ocean's resources.	
06	He tried to __________ how she should complete her project work.	
07	He began to __________ over his words during the speech.	
08	"Finding a coin on the ground was an __________ surprise."	
09	She tried to __________ the angry customer with a refund.	
10	His __________ efforts finally paid off.	
11	The scent of flowers was __________ throughout the garden.	
12	The judge will __________ over the trial next week.	
13	The __________ of the ancient wall stood in the middle of the field.	
14	The church is a __________ place for worship.	
15	They had to __________ through the snow to get home.	

A	Vanquish	B	Furthermore	C	Delirious	D	Devastate	E	Marred
F	Inhibit	G	Momentous	H	Recuperation	I	Consensus	J	Correspondence
K	Empathy	L	Diffuse	M	Ooze	N	Heed	O	Hasten

WK28	Exercise 28B	Answer
01	The group reached a __________ on the matter.	
02	Their __________ was frequent and friendly.	
03	He was __________ with joy when he heard the good news.	
04	The flood threatened to __________ the entire town.	
05	The light from the lamp helped __________ the darkness.	
06	She showed __________ towards those affected by the tragedy.	
07	The weather was cold; __________, it started to rain.	
08	They tried to __________ their departure to avoid the storm.	
09	He did not __________ the warning signs and got lost.	
10	"Loud noises can __________ you from thinking clearly."	
11	The surface was __________ by deep scratches.	
12	His graduation was a __________ occasion for his family.	
13	The wound began to __________ blood, causing concern.	
14	His __________ after surgery took several weeks.	
15	They were determined to __________ their rivals in the competition.	

11+ Vocabulary

Test B

A	Listlessness	B	Steadfast	C	Sentiment	D	Rescind	E	Luminary
F	Docile	G	Precedent	H	Succinct	I	Abyss	J	Placate
K	Commodity	L	Desolate	M	Imperious	N	Accountable	O	Excess

WK29	Exercise 29B	Answer
01	He peered down into the dark __________ with trepidation.	
02	She was __________ for the success of the project.	
03	Oil is a valuable __________ in the world.	
04	The __________ landscape stretched out for miles.	
05	The puppy was __________ and easy to train.	
06	The __________ food was donated to the local shelter.	
07	His __________ tone made others wary of him.	
08	She experienced __________ after being ill for days.	
09	The scientist was considered a __________ in her field.	
10	He tried to __________ his friend with a sincere apology.	
11	The court's ruling set a new legal __________.	
12	The company had to __________ the job offer due to budget cuts.	
13	The letter expressed his __________ of gratitude.	
14	She remained __________ in her commitment to the cause.	
15	His report was __________ and to the point.	

A	Proximity	B	Prestigious	C	Spurn	D	Resistance	E	Forthright
F	Covet	G	Designate	H	Procure	I	Wince	J	Simmer
K	Derelict	L	Exacerbate	M	Ramification	N	Pragmatic	O	Bereft

WK30	Exercise 30B	Answer
01	She felt __________ of hope after the loss.	
02	He couldn't help but __________ his neighbour's new car.	
03	The old, __________ house was an eyesore on the street.	
04	"The teacher will __________ the different teams for the game."	
05	His comments served to __________ the situation.	
06	She was __________ in expressing her opinion.	
07	His __________ approach led to quick solutions.	
08	He won a __________ award for his research.	
09	She managed to __________ the necessary materials for the project.	
10	The store's __________ to the house made it convenient.	
11	They considered the potential __________ of the decision.	
12	There was __________ to the new policies from employees.	
13	She let the soup __________ on the stove for hours.	
14	He decided to __________ the offer and pursue other opportunities.	
15	She couldn't help but __________ when she stubbed her toe.	

A	Despicable	B	Lout	C	Gullible	D	Disparate	E	Tandem
F	Noble	G	Premise	H	Transient	I	Covert	J	Aversion
K	Hitherto	L	Exposure	M	Stark	N	Rift	O	Strive

WK31	Exercise 31B	Answer
01	He had an __________ to spicy food and avoided it.	
02	The __________ operation was carried out with precision.	
03	His actions were considered __________ by many.	
04	Their __________ opinions made it hard to agree.	
05	Her __________ to the elements caused her to fall ill.	
06	He was __________ and easily fell for scams.	
07	She had __________ been unaware of the issue.	
08	His behaviour was that of a rude __________.	
09	The __________ cause rallied support from many.	
10	The __________ of the book intrigued her.	
11	The argument caused a __________ between the friends.	
12	The __________ contrast in their views led to heated debates.	
13	He continued to __________ for excellence in his work.	
14	The two worked in __________ to complete the project.	
15	His __________ lifestyle made it hard to keep a steady job.	

A	Perplexed	B	Paradox	C	Analogy	D	Antipathy	E	Poignant
F	Prodigy	G	Tyrant	H	Preservation	I	Augment	J	Solidarity
K	Galvanise	L	Commute	M	Productive	N	Poultry	O	Interrogate

WK32	Exercise 32B	Answer
01	He used an __________ to explain the complex concept.	
02	She felt an __________ toward the new policy.	
03	They hoped to __________ their income with part-time jobs.	
04	He had a long __________ to work every day.	
05	The news helped __________ the team into action.	
06	The detective had to __________ the suspect further.	
07	It was a __________ that the more he worked, the less he achieved.	
08	She was __________ by the unexpected turn of events.	
09	The movie's __________ ending left everyone in tears.	
10	They raised __________ on their farm for fresh eggs and meat.	
11	The __________ of historic buildings is important to the community.	
12	He was considered a musical __________ from a young age.	
13	The meeting was __________, resulting in a detailed plan.	
14	They showed __________ with the striking workers.	
15	The __________ ruled the kingdom with an iron fist.	

A	Esteem	B	Shelter	C	Renounce	D	Unanimous	E	Extreme
F	Subterfuge	G	Angst	H	Plight	I	Conscientious	J	Catastrophic
K	Colloquial	L	Feasible	M	Haughty	N	Charred	O	Expedite

WK33	Exercise 33B	Answer
01	The teenager expressed __________ over the uncertainty of the future.	
02	The hurricane caused __________ damage to the area.	
03	The fire left the building __________ and unrecognizable.	
04	"A __________ expression is an everyday way of speaking."	
05	She was __________ in her work and paid attention to detail.	
06	He held his mentor in high __________ for their guidance.	
07	She asked them to __________ the delivery of the package.	
08	The __________ heat made it difficult to work outside.	
09	It is __________ to complete the project by the deadline.	
10	His __________ attitude alienated others.	
11	They found themselves in a difficult __________ with little support.	
12	He decided to __________ his title and live a quiet life.	
13	They sought __________ from the storm in a nearby cabin.	
14	His __________ was discovered, and he was removed from his position.	
15	The council reached a __________ decision on the proposal.	

A	Concur	B	Auspicious	C	Scrutinize	D	Forfeit	E	Deluge
F	Trench	G	Procedures	H	Prohibit	I	Seclusion	J	Privilege
K	Beguiled	L	Archive	M	Grimace	N	Intercede	O	Bonus

WK34	Exercise 34B	Answer
01	The documents were placed in the __________ for safekeeping.	
02	The new year started with an __________ event.	
03	She was __________ by his charming personality.	
04	The team received a __________ for meeting their targets.	
05	I __________ with your assessment of the situation.	
06	The city experienced a __________ of rain during the storm.	
07	He had to __________ the match due to an injury.	
08	She couldn't help but __________ when she tasted the bitter medicine.	
09	He offered to __________ on behalf of his friend.	
10	It was a __________ to meet the renowned artist.	
11	"Safety __________ are rules we follow to stay safe."	
12	The law will __________ smoking in public areas.	
13	They will __________ the contract before signing it.	
14	He sought __________ in the mountains to clear his mind.	
15	The soldiers dug a __________ for protection during the battle.	

A	Notoriety	B	Imprudent	C	Hideous	D	Remonstrate	E	Precipitate
F	Contempt	G	Melee	H	Nominate	I	Hoarse	J	Congenial
K	Incessant	L	Deft	M	Elusive	N	Simultaneously	O	Edifice

WK35	Exercise 35B	Answer
01	The __________ atmosphere made everyone feel welcome.	
02	She looked at him with __________ after the argument.	
03	His __________ hands made quick work of the clay modelling project.	
04	The __________ towered over the surrounding buildings.	
05	The criminal remained __________ despite the police search.	
06	The painting was considered __________ by many.	
07	His voice was __________ from shouting all day.	
08	It would be __________ to make a decision without more information.	
09	The __________ noise made it difficult to concentrate.	
10	The __________ broke out suddenly and caught everyone off guard.	
11	She was __________d for the position by her colleagues.	
12	The actor gained __________ for his controversial comments.	
13	The sudden drop in temperature may __________ a snowstorm.	
14	She tried to __________ with him about his behaviour.	
15	They all spoke __________, creating a chaotic scene.	

A	Copious	B	Heralded	C	Compassion	D	Commemorate	E	Align
F	Charisma	G	Superficial	H	Rugged	I	Contradiction	J	Provocative
K	Transaction	L	Succumb	M	Altercation	N	Awry	O	Accustom

WK36	Exercise 36B	Answer
01	It took time to __________ herself to the new schedule.	
02	They worked to __________ their goals with the company's mission.	
03	The __________ between the two neighbours was quickly resolved.	
04	The plans went __________ when the weather took a turn for the worse.	
05	His __________ won him many supporters.	
06	They held a ceremony to __________ the event.	
07	She showed __________ to the injured animal.	
08	His statements were a __________ to the facts.	
09	He took __________ notes during the lecture.	
10	The new product was __________ as a breakthrough in technology.	
11	His __________ comments stirred up controversy.	
12	The __________ terrain made the journey challenging.	
13	They did not __________ to the pressure of the opposition.	
14	The inspection was __________ and missed key issues.	
15	The __________ was completed smoothly and efficiently.	

A	Aesthetic	B	Adverse	C	Squander	D	Tendency	E	Respective
F	Affable	G	Concession	H	Translucent	I	Spurious	J	Glamorous
K	Exacting	L	Stagnant	M	Illiterate	N	Resilience	O	Deficiency

WK37	Exercise 37B	Answer
01	They faced __________ weather conditions during the hike.	
02	The room had a calming __________ that made it inviting.	
03	His __________ nature made him a popular host.	
04	They reached a __________ to end the dispute.	
05	The test results revealed a __________ in the soil.	
06	Her __________ standards made her a successful manager.	
07	The event was __________ and attended by celebrities.	
08	She worked to teach reading skills to __________ adults.	
09	His __________ helped him overcome many challenges.	
10	They returned to their __________ homes after the event.	
11	The evidence provided was found to be __________.	
12	He was known to __________ his money on unnecessary things.	
13	The __________ water was a breeding ground for mosquitoes.	
14	She had a __________ to procrastinate on difficult tasks.	
15	The glass was __________, allowing light to pass through.	

A	Scope	B	Apportion	C	Strident	D	Stealth	E	Curtail
F	Substantial	G	Sag	H	Falter	I	Repercussions	J	Redundant
K	Amass	L	Assiduous	M	Clasp	N	Precocious	O	Idyllic

WK38	Exercise 38B	Answer
01	He managed to __________ a large collection of books over the years.	
02	They decided to __________ the tasks equally among the team.	
03	His __________ work ethic earned him a promotion.	
04	She used a __________ to secure the necklace around her neck.	
05	They had to __________ their vacation due to an emergency.	
06	He did not __________ in his determination to succeed.	
07	They spent an __________ afternoon by the lake.	
08	The child was considered __________ for his advanced vocabulary.	
09	The company had to eliminate __________ positions.	
10	They had to deal with the __________ of their decision.	
11	The old couch began to __________ in the middle.	
12	"The __________ of the project is how big or small it will be."	
13	The cat moved with __________ through the tall grass.	
14	Her __________ voice could be heard across the room.	
15	They made __________ progress on the project.	

11+ Vocabulary

A	Swindle	B	Tirade	C	Burgeon	D	Precede	E	Triumph
F	Compile	G	Indiscriminate	H	Perspire	I	Sanctuary	J	Garble
K	Vocation	L	Frugal	M	Audacious	N	Quagmire	O	Tedious

WK39	Exercise 39B	Answer
01	His ___________ plan was met with scepticism.	
02	The plants began to ___________ with the arrival of spring.	
03	She had to ___________ all the data into a single report.	
04	Her ___________ habits helped her save a lot of money.	
05	His speech was ___________d due to a bad connection.	
06	The fire spread ___________ly through the forest.	
07	He began to ___________ under the hot sun.	
08	The introduction will ___________ the main presentation.	
09	They found themselves in a legal ___________.	
10	The ___________ provided a safe haven for wildlife.	
11	He tried to ___________ the old woman out of her savings.	
12	The task was ___________, but necessary to complete.	
13	The manager's ___________ left everyone feeling uncomfortable.	
14	They celebrated their ___________ with a grand party.	
15	She found her true ___________ as a teacher.	

A	Pinnacle	B	Effervescent	C	Prominent	D	Conducive	E	Heedless
F	Delegate	G	Reluctant	H	Dither	I	Induce	J	Preposterous
K	Chastised	L	Brooding	M	Brusque	N	Capacity	O	Avert

WK40	Exercise 40B	Answer
01	They worked quickly to ___________ a crisis.	
02	His ___________ demeanour worried his friends.	
03	His ___________ manner made people feel uneasy.	
04	The room reached its full ___________ during the event.	
05	He was ___________ for his poor performance.	
06	The quiet environment was ___________ to studying.	
07	He decided to ___________ some tasks to his team.	
08	She began to ___________ over which option to choose.	
09	Her ___________ personality made her a joy to be around.	
10	He was ___________ of the warning signs and got lost.	
11	"The funny joke can ___________ laughter."	
12	His career reached its ___________ with the award.	
13	His ___________ idea was quickly dismissed.	
14	The statue was a ___________ feature in the town square.	
15	He was ___________ to take on the extra work.	

A	Convoluted	B	Exalt	C	Penchant	D	Euphoria	E	Thrifty
F	Construe	G	Suppress	H	Invade	I	Consistency	J	Bemoan
K	Culpable	L	Inept	M	Antagonistic	N	Flamboyant	O	Debilitate

WK41	Exercise 41B	Answer
01	His __________ behaviour caused tension in the group.	
02	She would often __________ the loss of her childhood.	
03	__________ in her performance earned her a promotion.	
04	It's important to __________ the message accurately.	
05	The __________ story was difficult to follow.	
06	He was found __________ for the accident.	
07	The illness began to __________ him over time.	
08	She felt a sense of __________ after receiving the news.	
09	They __________ the athlete for his remarkable achievements.	
10	His __________ style made him stand out in the crowd.	
11	His __________ handling of the situation led to further problems.	
12	The army planned to __________ the enemy's territory.	
13	He had a __________ for collecting rare books.	
14	The government sought to __________ the protests.	
15	She is __________ and always looks for the best deals.	

A	Conspicuous	B	Petrified	C	Quandary	D	Accolade	E	Barbaric
F	Diligent	G	Corroborate	H	Frenetic	I	Faux	J	Tentative
K	Wretched	L	Zenith	M	Flattery	N	Sociable	O	Captivity

WK42	Exercise 42B	Answer
01	The author received an __________ for her latest novel.	
02	The __________ practices were condemned by many.	
03	The animal suffered in __________ for many years.	
04	The __________ sign caught everyone's attention.	
05	The witness was able to __________ the suspect's story.	
06	He is __________ in his work and always meets deadlines.	
07	She saw through his __________ and remained cautious.	
08	He was __________ at the sight of the large spider.	
09	She found herself in a __________ over which path to take.	
10	Her __________ nature made her popular at parties.	
11	He took a __________ step toward the edge of the cliff.	
12	He felt __________ after his team's defeat.	
13	His career reached its __________ with his latest project.	
14	The __________ pace of the city exhausted her.	
15	He wore a __________ fur jacket to the event.	

Test B

A	Impair	B	Indifferent	C	Retribution	D	Camaraderie	E	Comprehensive
F	Subside	G	Plump	H	Uncouth	I	Vindictive	J	Viable
K	Fictitious	L	Contemporary	M	Sturdy	N	Ingenious	O	Condone

WK43	Exercise 43B	Answer
01	The team had strong __________ after working together for years.	
02	The __________ report covered all aspects of the issue.	
03	The manager could not __________ his employees' tardiness.	
04	They prefer __________ art over classical pieces.	
05	The story was a __________ account of the events.	
06	The injury began to __________ his ability to work.	
07	She remained __________ to the outcome of the game.	
08	His __________ solution solved the complex problem.	
09	The baby was __________ and healthy.	
10	He sought __________ for the harm done to him.	
11	The __________ table supported the heavy load.	
12	The storm began to __________ after a few hours.	
13	His __________ behaviour offended the guests.	
14	They found a __________ solution to the issue.	
15	His __________ actions caused trouble for others.	

A	Competent	B	Exhort	C	Animosity	D	Beleaguered	E	Disparaging
F	Compensation	G	Perilous	H	Exonerate	I	Content	J	Prosperous
K	Replenish	L	Fortuitous	M	Deplore	N	Imperative	O	Conservation

WK44	Exercise 44B	Answer
01	The __________ between the two teams was evident.	
02	"He felt __________ when he had to do too many tasks at once."	
03	He received __________ for the damages caused.	
04	She is __________ in her job and handles tasks efficiently.	
05	They work on __________ efforts to protect wildlife.	
06	He was __________ with his simple life in the countryside.	
07	Many people __________ the destruction of the rainforest.	
08	The coach would __________ his team to give their best effort.	
09	He was __________d from the charges against him.	
10	Their meeting was __________ and led to a great partnership.	
11	It is __________ to follow the safety instructions.	
12	The journey was __________ due to rough terrain.	
13	They lived a __________ life after their business succeeded.	
14	He had to __________ the water supply for his plants.	
15	His __________ remarks upset the audience.	

Test B

A	Enigmatic	B	Plausible	C	Strategy	D	Reprimand	E	Bane
F	Captivating	G	Substantiate	H	Epiphany	I	Reform	J	Bureaucracy
K	Incredulous	L	Apoplectic	M	Relapse	N	Segment	O	Turmoil

WK45	Exercise 45B	Answer
01	He became __________ when he learned of the mistake.	
02	The weeds were the __________ of the gardener's existence.	
03	The __________ caused delays in the process.	
04	Her __________ performance earned a standing ovation.	
05	The years of war had left the region in a state of __________.	
06	He was __________ at the unexpected news.	
07	Her explanation seemed __________ to the investigators.	
08	They sought to __________ the outdated policies.	
09	The patient experienced a __________ in his condition.	
10	The manager had to __________ the employee for being late.	
11	The presentation was divided into several __________s.	
12	They planned a __________ to improve their sales.	
13	The evidence was used to __________ his claims.	
14	Her __________ smile left him curious about her thoughts.	
15	He had an __________ that changed his perspective on life.	

A	Opulence	B	Withdraw	C	Ritual	D	Insightful	E	Benevolent
F	Forthcoming	G	Composure	H	Exempt	I	Hoist	J	Odious
K	Contrite	L	Differentiate	M	Lauded	N	Dissipate	O	Patronising

WK46	Exercise 46B	Answer
01	She is known for her __________ acts of charity.	
02	He maintained his __________ during the stressful meeting.	
03	He was __________ for his previous mistakes and apologized.	
04	It's important to __________ between the two options.	
05	The fog began to __________ as the sun rose.	
06	She was __________ from the new rules due to her seniority.	
07	He was __________ about the challenges they faced.	
08	They had to __________ the heavy equipment onto the truck.	
09	Her __________ analysis provided valuable information.	
10	He was __________ for his contributions to the community.	
11	The __________ smell made it hard to breathe.	
12	The mansion was a display of his __________.	
13	His __________ tone upset the employees.	
14	"Reading a bedtime story is a nice evening __________."	
15	She decided to __________ from the competition.	

A	Tantamount	B	Unequivocal	C	Inferno	D	Presume	E	Disseminate
F	Torrid	G	Tributary	H	Constitute	I	Abbreviate	J	Detrimental
K	Ascertain	L	Demure	M	Impoverished	N	Concerted	O	Implore

WK47	Exercise 47B	Answer
01	"We can __________ the word 'television' to 'TV'."	
02	He tried to __________ the cause of the problem.	
03	They made a __________ effort to complete the project.	
04	"Plants, animals, and humans __________ the living things on Earth."	
05	Her __________ demeanour made a positive impression.	
06	Smoking is __________ to your health.	
07	They worked to __________ information to the public.	
08	He began to __________ them for mercy.	
09	The __________ community needed support.	
10	The fire turned into a raging __________ that engulfed the forest.	
11	I __________ you will attend the meeting tomorrow.	
12	His resignation is __________ to admitting guilt.	
13	The __________ heat of the desert was unbearable.	
14	The __________ flowed into the main river, nourishing the land.	
15	The evidence against him was __________ and clear.	

A	Reiterate	B	Imitate	C	Obliterate	D	Fundamentally	E	Probe
F	Counterpart	G	Heave	H	Debrief	I	Ferocity	J	Cultivate
K	Profound	L	Gallant	M	Trait	N	Drowsy	O	Depot

WK48	Exercise 48B	Answer
01	His __________ in the other department is just as efficient.	
02	They worked hard to __________ their garden and grow fresh vegetables.	
03	After the mission, they gathered to __________ and discuss the outcomes.	
04	The supplies were stored in the __________ for future use.	
05	He felt __________ after taking the medication.	
06	The __________ of the storm took everyone by surprise.	
07	They __________ disagreed on the approach to the project.	
08	His __________ efforts during the crisis were recognized by the community.	
09	He had to __________ the heavy box onto the truck.	
10	The child loved to __________ the actions of her older sibling.	
11	The tornado threatened to __________ the small town.	
12	They decided to __________ deeper into the matter to find the truth.	
13	The lecture left a __________ impact on the students.	
14	She had to __________ the instructions to ensure everyone understood.	
15	His kindness is one of his most admirable __________s.	

A	Debunk	B	Picturesque	C	Potential	D	Exemplary	E	Architecture
F	Vilify	G	Cascade	H	Duress	I	Assuage	J	Frivolous
K	Interim	L	Relegate	M	Taxing	N	Prevail	O	Miscellaneous

WK49	Exercise 49B	Answer
01	The ___________ of the cathedral was stunning.	
02	She tried to ___________ his fears by offering reassurance.	
03	The water flowed down the ___________ into the pond below.	
04	They worked to ___________ the myths surrounding the event.	
05	He made the confession under ___________, so it was deemed invalid.	
06	His ___________ conduct earned him high praise.	
07	She was known for her ___________ spending habits.	
08	He will serve as the ___________ manager until a permanent replacement is found.	
09	She packed ___________ items into the last box.	
10	The ___________ village was surrounded by rolling hills.	
11	The young athlete showed great ___________ in his sport.	
12	The team worked hard to ___________ in the final match.	
13	The company decided to ___________ the project to a lower priority.	
14	The job was both physically and mentally ___________.	
15	The media tried to ___________ the politician for his controversial statements.	

A	Derail	B	Prolific	C	Clout	D	Hypocritical	E	Illusive
F	Crestfallen	G	Escalate	H	Cynic	I	Archaic	J	Lease
K	Defame	L	Foreboding	M	Marina	N	Scrooge	O	Conciliatory

WK50	Exercise 50B	Answer
01	The building's design was considered ___________ and needed renovation.	
02	He had a lot of ___________ in the business world and could get things done.	
03	Her ___________ tone helped ease the tension in the room.	
04	He was ___________ when he didn't get the promotion.	
05	He was a ___________ and rarely believed anything without evidence.	
06	They tried to ___________ the celebrity with false accusations.	
07	The sudden change of plans threatened to ___________ their project.	
08	The argument began to ___________ quickly, causing concern.	
09	A sense of ___________ hung in the air as the storm approached.	
10	His ___________ stance on the issue upset many people.	
11	The ___________ animal remained hidden from view.	
12	He decided to ___________ the apartment for a year.	
13	They kept their boat at the local ___________.	
14	The ___________ author published multiple books each year.	
15	He was considered a ___________ due to his stingy behaviour.	

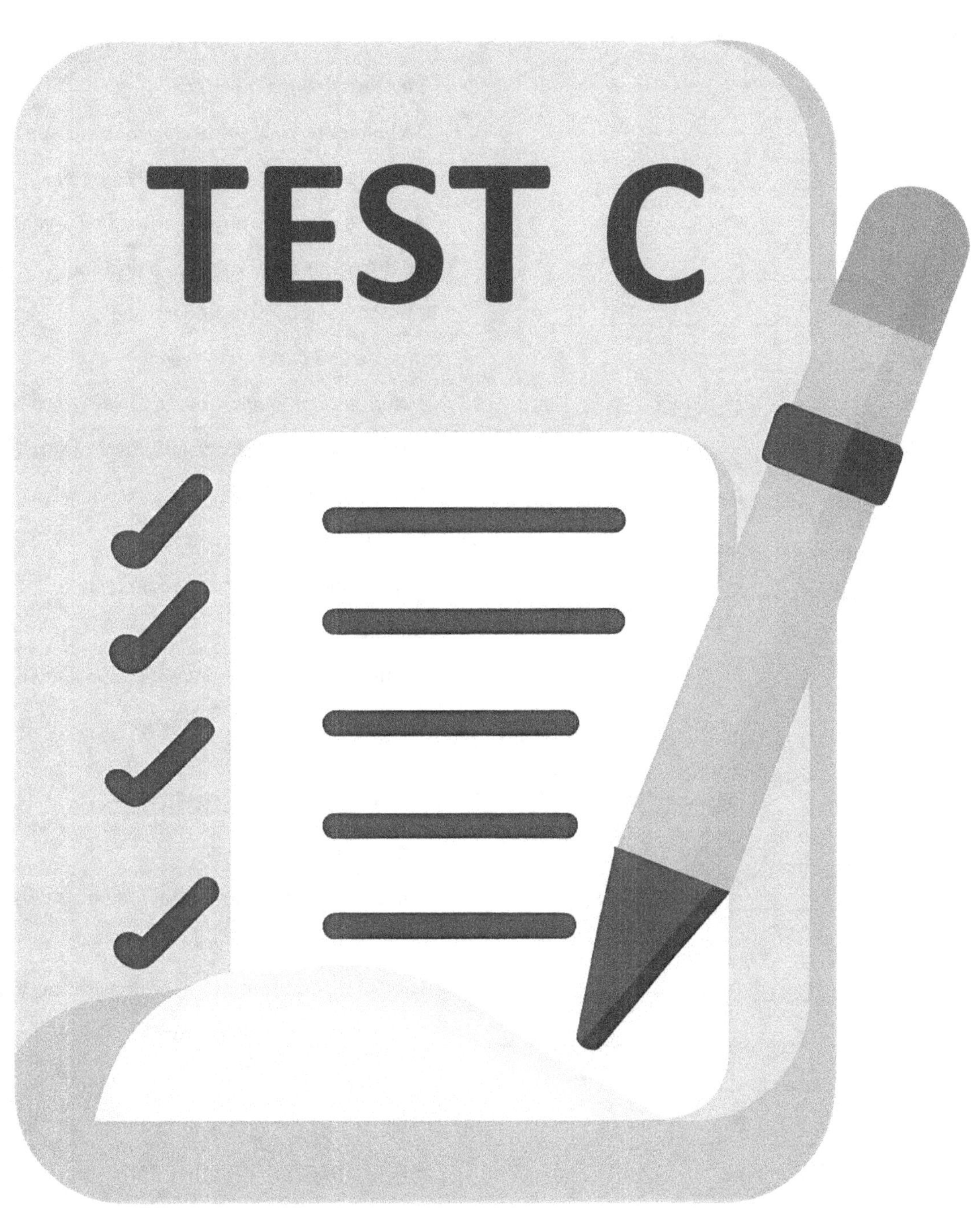
TEST C

Test C

Refer to the corresponding week for answers (pages 1 to 50)

WK01	Word	Definition
01	f __ __ __ __ e	Pointless, having no effect
02	m __ __ __ c	To imitate or copy the actions of someone or something
03	p __ __ __ __ __ __ t	To prolong for an unnecessarily long time
04	c __ __ __ __ s	A severe problem or danger needing urgent attention
05	c __ __ __ __ r	To discuss in order to reach a decision
06	d __ __ __ __ __ __ __ __ __ e	Able to be noticed or understood
07	f __ __ __ __ __ r	Intense and passionate feeling
08	d __ __ __ __ __ __ __ t	Luxurious, indulgent, or excessively rich
09	t __ __ __ __ __ n	A stretch of land, especially with regard to its features
10	h __ __ __ __ e	Move very quickly and often uncontrollably
11	s __ __ __ __ __ y	Of food: salty or spicy, not sweet
12	c __ __ __ __ __ __ __ t	Happening all the time or repeatedly
13	p __ __ __ __ __ __ __ e	Delay until later
14	p __ __ __ __ __ __ __ __ __ __ __ __ __ l	Relating to the study of wisdom and knowledge
15	n __ __ __ __ __ s	A long-standing rival or enemy

WK02	Word	Definition
01	w __ __ __ h	Extreme anger
02	c __ __ __ __ __ __ __ __ c	Releasing strong emotions in a cleansing way
03	m __ __ __ __ __ __ l	Expressing sorrow or grief
04	c __ __ __ __ __ __ r	Loud and persistent noise, often with shouting
05	u __ __ __ __ __ __ __ __ __ __ __ __ d	Never done or known before
06	c __ __ __ __ __ __ __ __ __ e	The act of following rules or commands
07	s __ __ __ __ d	Having sharp powers of judgment
08	s __ __ m	A poor, overcrowded urban area
09	f __ __ __ __ __ __ __ t	Not serious, showing a lack of respect
10	r __ __ __ __ n	A fixed amount of something allowed due to short supply
11	d __ __ __ __ __ e	Hate strongly
12	i __ __ __ __ __ __ __ __ __ __ __ __ __ e	Impossible to overcome
13	c __ __ __ __ e	Feel embarrassed or disgusted
14	m __ __ __ __ __ r	To follow a winding path
15	a __ __ __ __ __ h	Extreme suffering and distress

Test C

WK03	Word	Definition
01	c _ _ _ _ _ e	A close friend
02	s _ _ _ n	Strict and severe
03	a _ _ _ _ _ _ _ _ _ r	A person representing their country in a foreign place
04	h _ _ _ _ _ _ e	Cultural traditions or features passed down from the past
05	c _ _ _ _ _ _ _ n	A temporary group formed for a goal
06	n _ _ _ _ _ _ _ e	A story or account of events
07	C _ _ _ _ _ _ _ e	To have a close connection between two things
08	d _ _ _ _ _ _ _ _ s	People who criticize something strongly
09	a _ _ _ _ _ _ _ _ d	Outdated or no longer in use
10	p _ _ _ _ _ _ _ _ _ _ _ _ y	Mainly or mostly
11	a _ _ _ _ t	Although or even though
12	i _ _ _ _ _ _ _ _ _ _ _ _ _ e	Absolutely necessary
13	c _ _ _ _ _ _ _ _ y	People living in a shared area
14	s _ _ _ _ _ _ m	The use of irony to mock or convey contempt
15	v _ _ d	Completely empty; invalid

WK04	Word	Definition
01	p _ _ _ _ _ _ a	A large or excessive amount of something
02	f _ _ _ d	An evil or wicked person
03	p _ _ _ _ _ _ _ _ e	Happening too soon, before the proper time
04	t _ _ _ _ _ _ _ _ e	To occur or happen
05	d _ _ _ _ h	A scarcity or lack of something
06	d _ _ _ _ _ e	Showing a lot of variety
07	t _ _ _ e	Brief and to the point
08	c _ _ _ _ _ _ _ _ _ n	A disagreement or conflict
09	s _ _ _ c	Enduring hardship without showing emotion
10	a _ _ _ _ r	Enthusiasm or passion
11	v _ _ _ d	Bright and distinct; producing strong mental images
12	r _ _ _ _ d	Smelling or tasting unpleasant
13	c _ _ _ _ _ l	Warm and friendly
14	i _ _ _ _ _ e	To completely cover in liquid, or to deeply involve oneself
15	a _ _ _ _ _ _ _ n	Excessive praise or admiration

WK05	Word	Definition
01	d _ _ _ _ _ _ _ _ e	Delightful, especially of food
02	p _ _ _ _ _ _ _ _ _ _ r	A person who held a job or office before the current person
03	i _ _ _ _ _ _ _ _ _ _ e	Include as a part of something larger
04	n _ _ _ _ e	A subtle difference or variation
05	p _ _ _ _ _ _ _ d	Disturbed, feeling anxious or unsettled
06	d _ _ _ _ e	An official order or decision
07	d _ _ _ _ _ e	Treat with disrespect or make worse
08	e _ _ _ _ _ _ c	Feeling extreme happiness
09	d _ _ _ _ _ _ _ y	Deceitfulness or double-dealing
10	t _ _ _ t	To contaminate or pollute something
11	s _ _ _ e	To push forcefully
12	r _ _ _ _ _ _ _ _ _ _ y	Basic or undeveloped
13	p _ _ _ _ _ t	Wise, careful in making decisions
14	l _ _ _ d	Clear and easy to understand
15	C _ _ _ _ _ _ _ e	To move around or spread

WK06	Word	Definition
01	s _ _ _ _ _ _ _ e	A sudden rush of panicked animals or people
02	p _ _ _ _ _ l	Crucially important
03	m _ _ _ _ _ y	Hoarding money and reluctant to spend
04	p _ _ _ _ _ e	Stealing violently, especially in a time of war
05	d _ _ _ _ _ _ y	Disorder or confusion
06	g _ _ _ _ _ _ _ _ _ s	Sociable and enjoying the company of others
07	p _ _ _ _ _ _ _ e	So intense it's almost physically felt
08	m _ _ _ _ _ _ _ _ _ t	Having ill intentions or wishing harm upon others
09	c _ _ _ _ _ t	An idea or understanding
10	e _ _ _ _ _ e	The fundamental nature or most important quality of something
11	b _ _ _ _ n	Gentle or kind; not harmful
12	h _ _ _ _ _ r	A port, or a place of shelter & safety
13	r _ _ _ _ _ _ s	Extremely hungry
14	a _ _ _ _ _ _ _ _ _ _ e	Able to express ideas clearly and fluently
15	f _ _ _ _ _ e	Skilful and delicate handling of a situation

Test C

Refer to the corresponding week for answers (pages 1 to 50)

WK07	Word	Definition
01	s __ __ __ n	The feeling that someone or something is worthless or despicable
02	v __ __ __ __ __ __ t	Decision e.g. On a court case
03	a __ __ __ __ __ __ __ __ e	Make pain or suffering less severe
04	e __ __ __ __ __ t	Show something publicly (like in a museum)
05	s __ __ __ __ __ s	Exceed or be greater than
06	t __ __ __ __ __ __ __ y	The quality of being determined or persistent
07	c __ __ __ __ __ __ __ __ __ __ __ n	A group of people gathered for religious worship
08	i __ __ __ __ __ __ __ __ e	The occurrence or frequency of something
09	p __ __ __ __ __ __ c	Excessively concerned with minor details or rules
10	p __ __ __ __ __ __ __ __ __ __ __ __ n	Rapid increase in number
11	g __ __ __ e	Measure or estimate
12	n __ __ __ __ __ __ __ t	Failing to take care
13	i __ __ __ __ __ __ __ l	Fair, not taking sides
14	r __ __ d	The tough outer layer or skin of certain fruits or cheeses
15	a __ __ __ __ __ __ __ y	Unfairly chosen; based on chance rather than reason

WK08	Word	Definition
01	c __ __ __ __ __ __ __ __ __ __ __ l	Arranged in the order things happened
02	c __ __ __ __ __ __ n	A series of actions to achieve a goal
03	s __ __ __ __ __ __ e	Soak thoroughly
04	s __ __ __ __ __ __ __ __ __ t	Something added to complete a thing
05	r __ __ __ __ __ __ d	Famous and well-known
06	s __ __ __ __ __ __ __ l	Not easily convinced; having doubts or reservations
07	s __ __ __ __ __ __ e	Go beneath the surface of water
08	c __ __ __ __ __ r	The quality of being honest and open
09	g __ __ __ __ __ o	Enthusiastic and eager
10	p __ __ __ __ __ __ __ __ n	A remarkable fact or occurrence
11	p __ __ __ __ __ l	A hidden or unsuspected danger or difficulty
12	r __ __ __ __ __ __ __ __ __ n	A firm decision to do or not to do something
13	o __ __ __ __ __ __ __ __ __ __ g	Intense and difficult to resist
14	p __ __ __ __ __ a	The image a person presents to the public
15	p __ __ __ __ t	Having a strong effect or influence

Test C

Refer to the corresponding week for answers (pages 1 to 50)

WK09	Word	Definition
01	e _ _ _ _ _ _ _ e	An area surrounded by a fence or barrier
02	p _ _ _ _ _ _ _ _ _ _ t	A difficult, unpleasant, or embarrassing situation
03	e _ _ _ _ _ e	Come from a source (light, smell, etc.)
04	p _ _ _ _ _ _ _ _ _ n	A paid job that requires specialized training
05	i _ _ _ _ e	Encourage or provoke someone to do something, often violent
06	m _ _ _ _ _ _ k	An independent person, not following the usual way
07	o _ _ _ _ e	To do something as a favour or to meet a request
08	c _ _ t	Rudely brief or abrupt
09	r _ _ _ _ _ e	What's left behind after removing the main part
10	d _ _ _ _ _ _ _ e	Criticize or speak badly of someone
11	o _ _ _ t	Done or shown openly
12	s _ _ _ _ _ _ e	Being alone; without company
13	c _ _ _ _ _ n	To express strong disapproval or criticize severely
14	s _ _ _ _ _ _ _ _ _ t	Someone who spends money wastefully
15	s _ _ _ _ _ _ c	Occurring occasionally or irregularly

WK10	Word	Definition
01	m _ _ _ _ _ _ _ _ s	Dull and repetitive
02	f _ _ _ _ _ e	To abandon or give up on someone or something
03	a _ _ _ _ _ _ _ _ _ e	To gather or collect over time
04	t _ _ _ _ _ _ e	Perceptible by touch, real or concrete
05	t _ _ _ _ t	A student absent from school without permission
06	e _ _ _ _ _ _ s	To surround or include
07	c _ _ _ _ _ y	To confirm or guarantee something is true
08	p _ _ _ _ _ _ _ _ s	Unstable, likely to fall or collapse
09	v _ _ _ _ _ e	A risky journey or undertaking
10	P _ _ _ _ _ _ _ _ e	Recklessly extravagant or wasteful
11	a _ _ _ _ _ _ y	A natural liking or connection
12	a _ _ _ _ _ _ _ _ _ d	Completely destroyed or wiped out
13	l _ _ _ _ _ _ _ h	A complex and confusing network of passages
14	P _ _ _ _ _ _ _ _ e	To cause something to continue indefinitely
15	l _ _ _ _ _ _ h	To become weak or feeble

Test C

Refer to the corresponding week for answers (pages 1 to 50)

WK11	Word	Definition
01	i __ __ __ __ e	Fill something with a quality
02	r __ __ __ __ __ y	Easily, quickly, and willingly
03	s __ __ __ t	To walk with a proud, confident manner
04	c __ __ __ __ __ __ __ __ e	An agreement where each side gives in a bit
05	m __ __ __ __ __ __ e	To make less severe or harsh
06	a __ __ __ __ __ __ __ e	A quality or characteristic
07	d __ __ __ __ e	To mock or ridicule
08	d __ __ __ __ t	To make someone feel sad or hopeless
09	c __ __ __ __ __ __ y	The opposite
10	i __ __ __ __ __ __ __ __ s	Harmless and unlikely to cause offense
11	c __ __ __ __ __ __ __ l	Cheerful and sociable
12	j __ __ __ __ e	To push or bump against someone roughly
13	c __ __ __ __ __ d	To compete or argue
14	a __ __ __ __ __ __ __ __ __ e	To provoke or annoy someone
15	e __ __ __ __ __ __ __ __ e	Full of energy, excitement, and cheerfulness

WK12	Word	Definition
01	h __ __ __ __ d	A mix of two different things
02	e __ __ __ __ __ t	Stylish and sophisticated
03	r __ __ __ __ __ __ __ __ __ __ __ __ e	Deserving strong disapproval
04	c __ __ __ __ __ __ __ __ __ __ e	To work together on a project or task
05	w __ __ __ __ r	Become dry and shrivelled ; fade away
06	c __ __ __ __ __ __ __ __ __ __ e	To combine or strengthen
07	t __ __ __ __ __ __ __ __ d	A point of entry or beginning
08	r __ __ __ __ __ __ e	Delay or cancel a punishment
09	e __ __ __ __ __ __ __ __ d	Involved deeply in an argument or conflict
10	p __ __ __ __ __ s	A series of steps to achieve something
11	j __ __ __ __ l	Cheerful and friendly
12	s __ __ __ __ __ __ __ __ __ e	Likely to be influenced or harmed
13	p __ __ __ __ __ __ __ y	Mainly or chiefly
14	r __ __ __ __ t	Withdraw a statement or promise
15	c __ __ __ __ __ __ t	Clearly expressed and easy to understand

Test C

WK13	Word	Definition
01	c _ _ _ _ _ _ t	A disagreement or fight
02	p _ _ _ _ _ d	To continue doing something
03	c _ _ _ _ _ _ _ _ _ _ e	Facial expression OR approval
04	b _ _ _ _ _ _ _ _ _ t	Hostile and aggressive
05	c _ _ _ _ _ c	Mysterious or puzzling
06	h _ _ _ _ s	A break or pause in activity
07	e _ _ _ _ _ _ _ n	Something not included in a general rule - a one-off
08	a _ _ _ _ _ _ _ _ _ n	Something causing pain or suffering
09	i _ _ _ _ _ _ _ _ e	To make something up as you go along
10	a _ _ _ _ _ _ _ e	Having a friendly and peaceful relationship
11	a _ _ _ _ _ n	To stop or postpone a meeting or activity
12	c _ _ _ _ _ _ _ _ d	Seeming artificial, forced, or unnatural
13	c _ _ _ _ _ _ _ _ _ _ _ e	The result of an action
14	s _ _ _ _ _ _ _ o	A possible sequence of events
15	c _ _ _ _ _ _ s	Uncaring about the feelings of others

WK14	Word	Definition
01	a _ _ _ _ _ _ _ _ s	Not clear or having more than one possible meaning
02	r _ _ _ _ _ _ _ _ _ t	Extremely distasteful or offensive
03	e _ _ _ _ _ _ t	Famous, respected, and distinguished
04	h _ _ _ _ _ s	Extremely wicked or evil
05	e _ _ _ _ _ _ m	Cry out suddenly because of strong emotion
06	e _ _ _ _ _ _ t	To take advantage of someone or something for personal gain
07	d _ _ _ _ _ _ _ _ e	Showing respect or politeness
08	s _ _ _ _ _ _ e	Be enough or adequate
09	b _ _ _ _ _ e	Easily broken or fragile
10	d _ _ _ _ _ s	Doubtful or uncertain
11	h _ _ e	Sharpen or make more effective
12	d _ _ _ _ t	To represent or show in a picture or words
13	a _ _ _ _ _ _ _ e	A person who supports or speaks in favour of something
14	i _ _ _ _ _ _ _ y	Honesty and moral principles
15	s _ _ _ _ _ _ _ _ _ _ _ _ e	Close observation, especially of a suspected spy or criminal

Refer to the corresponding week for answers (pages 1 to 50)

WK15	Word	Definition
01	c _ _ _ _ _ _ y	Mercy or forgiveness
02	h _ _ _ h	Severe, cruel, or unkind
03	s _ _ _ _ _ _ _ s	Requiring great effort or energy
04	v _ _ _ _ _ e	Using more words than needed; long-winded
05	o _ _ _ _ _ s	Giving the impression that something bad is going to happen
06	s _ _ _ _ _ d	Unusually quiet; lacking in energy
07	a _ _ _ _ _ _ _ e	Make someone feel isolated or unwelcome
08	c _ _ _ _ _ _ _ _ _ _ r	An expert with great taste, especially in art, food, etc.
09	a _ _ _ _ _ e	Tell or inform someone of something
10	p _ _ _ _ _ _ e	To prevent something from happening
11	p _ _ _ _ _ _ _ _ _ y	Happening before a more important event
12	b _ _ _ _ _ t	Able to float or cheerful and optimistic
13	d _ _ _ _ y	Dull, depressing, and boring
14	a _ _ _ _ _ e	Something old and valuable, usually from a past era
15	o _ _ _ _ _ _ _ e	Stubborn and refusing to change

WK16	Word	Definition
01	c _ _ _ _ _ y	Done quickly and without much attention to detail
02	m _ _ _ _ _ _ _ e	Average or unremarkable
03	c _ _ _ _ _ _ _ _ _ _ e	A guess based on incomplete information
04	p _ _ _ _ s	Having small holes that allow liquid or air to pass through
05	r _ _ _ _ e	To feel deep respect or admiration for something
06	d _ _ _ _ _ _ e	To force someone or something out of its usual place
07	c _ _ _ _ _ _ _ _ _ _ _ l	Following traditional or usual ways
08	n _ _ _ _ e	To nullify or make ineffective
09	p _ _ _ _ d	Calm and peaceful
10	m _ _ _ l	A very wealthy and powerful businessperson
11	i _ _ _ _ _ _ _ e	Point out or suggest something
12	f _ _ _ _ _ _ _ t	Openly and shockingly bad or offensive
13	e _ _ _ _ _ _ _ s	Special importance given to something
14	s _ _ _ _ _ _ _ _ e	Form a theory without firm evidence
15	a _ _ _ _ _ _ _ t	Wealthy or having a lot of resources

11+ Vocabulary

Test C

Refer to the corresponding week for answers (pages 1 to 50)

WK17	Word	Definition
01	C _ _ _ _ _ _ _ e	Destructive, able to wear away substances
02	d _ _ _ _ _ _ _ e	Extremely poor
03	l _ _ _ _ e	Responsible or likely to
04	c _ _ _ _ _ e	To tell someone a secret, trusting them
05	c _ _ _ _ _ _ _ _ n	A standard by which something is judged
06	t _ _ _ _ _ r	A fishing boat that uses a trawl net
07	r _ _ _ _ _ _ _ _ _ e	Open and willing to consider something
08	p _ _ _ _ t	To allow or give permission
09	p _ _ _ e	A cloud of smoke, steam, etc OR decorative feather or cluster of feathers
10	i _ _ _ _ _ _ _ _ _ _ _ t	Stopping and starting at intervals
11	r _ _ _ n	A strap for controlling a horse.
12	a _ _ _ _ _ _ _ _ _ _ e	Having mixed feelings or conflicting emotions
13	d _ _ _ _ _ t	Openly refusing to obey
14	c _ _ _ _ _ _ _ _ _ y	Involvement in something wrong
15	p _ _ _ _ _ _ _ m	To announce officially or publicly

WK18	Word	Definition
01	o _ _ _ _ _ _ _ _ s	Very unpleasant or offensive
02	c _ _ _ e	To cut into a shape
03	b _ _ _ _ d	Having a preference or prejudice
04	a _ _ _ _ _ _ d	Feeling troubled or disturbed
05	c _ _ _ _ _ _ _ _ _ _ e	Something that makes things easier
06	V _ _ _ _ _ _ _ _ s	Having a large appetite; very eager
07	r _ _ _ _ _ _ _ _ _ _ t	Reminding someone of something from the past
08	f _ _ _ _ _ _ _ _ _ s	Very careful about details, hard to please
09	p _ _ _ _ _ t	To fall or drop straight down at high speed
10	r _ _ _ _ e	Criticize sharply
11	s _ _ _ t	Sturdy and strong; somewhat fat
12	c _ _ _ _ _ e	A narrow crack or opening
13	s _ _ _ _ _ _ _ n	An individual example used for study or display
14	p _ _ _ _ e	To jump or fall suddenly
15	f _ _ _ _ _ _ _ e	Capable of making mistakes or being wrong

WK19	Word	Definition
01	e _ _ _ _ y	A feeling of intense hatred
02	d _ _ _ _ _ _ _ _ _ e	To decline in quality or character
03	e _ _ _ _ _ c	Irregular or unpredictable in movement or behaviour
04	t _ _ _ d	Lacking in self-assurance or courage; shy
05	p _ _ _ _ _ s	Arrogant, self-important
06	c _ _ _ _ _ _ _ _ _ e	Your inner sense of what's right and wrong
07	i _ _ _ _ _ _ _ t	About to happen very soon
08	b _ _ _ _ r	A protective barrier or cushion
09	r _ _ _ _ y	To formally approve or accept
10	r _ _ _ _ _ _ _ _ _ e	To strengthen or support with additional material
11	b _ _ k	Perform music or entertainment in a public place
12	c _ _ _ _ _ _ _ _ y	A secret plan to do something
13	f _ _ _ n	To pretend or fake
14	e _ _ _ _ _ _ _ _ _ _ g	Fascinating and captivating
15	d _ _ _ _ _ _ _ _ e	Formal discussion or writing on a topic

WK20	Word	Definition
01	c _ _ _ _ _ _ _ _ _ _ e	To think deeply about something
02	s _ _ _ _ _ _ d	Extremely dirty and unpleasant
03	v _ _ _ _ _ _ _ _ _ e	Open to attack, harm, or damage
04	i _ _ _ _ _ _ _ _ _ _ e	To secretly enter or become part of a group
05	r _ _ _ _ _ _ s	Having no pity or compassion
06	d _ _ _ _ _ _ _ _ e	Intending to mislead or trick
07	g _ _ _ e	To complain constantly
08	h _ _ _ _ e	Negotiate or argue about a price
09	h _ _ _ y	Able to survive difficult conditions
10	r _ _ _ _ e	Prove something false
11	f _ _ _ l	Wild or untamed, often referring to animals
12	s _ _ _ _ _ r	Walk in a slow, relaxed manner
13	q _ _ _ l	To suppress or put an end to something
14	c _ _ _ _ e	To force someone to do something
15	d _ _ _ _ _ _ _ c	Stubborn, unwilling to listen to others

Test C

WK21	Word	Definition
01	p _ _ _ _ _ _ e	The act of pretending or false appearance
02	f _ _ _ _ _ _ l	Absurd or ridiculous, often in a humorous way
03	p _ _ _ _ d	Rotten, foul-smelling
04	r _ _ _ _ _ _ _ e	Copy something exactly
05	a _ _ _ _ _ _ e	A short, amusing, or interesting story
06	r _ _ _ _ l	Expressing sorrow or regret in a slightly humorous way
07	e _ _ _ _ _ _ _ _ g	Charming and delightful
08	c _ _ _ _ _ _ _ l	Relating to the sky or outer space
09	h _ _ _ _ _ _ c	Clean and sanitary
10	d _ _ _ _ _ _ _ _ l	Extremely wicked or evil
11	d _ _ d	An action or accomplishment
12	i _ _ _ _ _ _ _ _ _ _ _ _ y	Accidentally, without intending to
13	f _ _ _ _ _ _ _ _ e	Not literal, using metaphor or simile
14	s _ _ _ _ _ _ _ _ _ _ s	Unnecessary; more than enough
15	a _ _ _ _ _ _ _ c	Unselfishly concerned for the wellbeing of others

WK22	Word	Definition
01	m _ _ _ _ _ _ m	The force or energy that keeps something moving
02	p _ _ _ _ t	Easily bent or flexible
03	i _ _ _ _ _ _ _ _ _ e	Flawless or perfect in every detail
04	i _ _ _ _ _ _ _ _ _ t	Confusing and unclear
05	i _ _ _ _ _ _ _ _ _ s	Unaffected or unable to be influenced
06	c _ _ _ _ l	To force someone to do something
07	n _ _ _ _ _ e	Care for and encourage growth
08	d _ _ _ _ _ e	Reveal a secret
09	p _ _ _ _ _ e	Any action that precedes something else.
10	c _ _ _ _ _ _ d	To confuse or surprise greatly
11	h _ _ _ _ s	Excessive pride and arrogance
12	a _ _ _ _ _ _ _ _ _ _ _ _ n	Favouring strict obedience to authority
13	d _ _ _ _ _ _ _ _ _ _ d	In very bad condition because of neglect
14	p _ _ _ _ _ _ _ t	Someone who expects the worst outcome
15	e _ _ _ _ _ _ _ c	Expressing something in a strong and forceful way

WK23

	Word	Definition
01	t _ _ _ _ _ _ _ _ _ e	Thin and worn out due to much use
02	b _ _ _ _ _ d	Puzzled, confused, or bewildered
03	m _ _ _ _ n	To speak badly of someone
04	p _ _ _ _ e	A solemn promise or commitment
05	s _ _ _ t	To divert or redirect
06	a _ _ _ _ _ _ _ _ _ _ s	When people argue in a mean and angry way
07	q _ _ _ _ _ _ _ _ e	Isolate due to disease risk
08	i _ _ _ _ _ _ _ _ u	Done without planning or preparation
09	i _ _ e	Inactive, not doing anything
10	c _ _ _ _ _ _ e	Belief that something is true
11	i _ _ _ _ _ _ t	Implied but not directly stated
12	d _ _ _ _ _ _ _ r	A person's behaviour or manner
13	u _ _ _ _ _ t	Having an untidy appearance
14	e _ _ _ _ _ _ t	Very clear and detailed, leaving no room for doubt
15	s _ _ _ _ _ _ _ s	Luxurious and expensive

WK24

	Word	Definition
01	i _ _ _ _ _ _ _ _ e	To frighten or threaten someone
02	d _ _ _ e	To search deeply or investigate thoroughly
03	n _ _ _ _ _ _ _ a	A sentimental longing for the past
04	m _ _ _ _ _ _ _ _ _ e	To interpret or understand wrongly
05	a _ _ _ _ _ _ _ t	Something you strongly dislike.
06	w _ _ _ _ _ _ _ l	Playfully quaint, especially in an appealing way
07	c _ _ _ _ _ _ _ _ e	Done by a group of people acting together
08	e _ _ _ _ _ _ h	To go past (exceed) your limit or boundary
09	s _ _ _ _ _ _ t	Strong, loyal, and reliable
10	c _ _ _ _ _ _ _ _ t	Satisfied with oneself, maybe too much so
11	m _ _ _ _ _ _ _ _ y	A feeling of deep sadness or sorrow
12	r _ _ _ _ _ _ _ s	Morally right or justifiable
13	s _ _ _ r	Clean or brighten by rubbing hard
14	p _ _ _ _ h	To die or be destroyed
15	c _ _ _ _ _ _ _ _ t	Limitation or restriction

WK25	Word	Definition
01	p _ _ _ _ _ _ _ e	A fundamental truth or rule
02	m _ _ _ _ _ e	Ordinary, not interesting or exciting
03	c _ _ _ _ _ _ t	Too much pride in oneself
04	s _ _ _ _ _ r	Run with quick light steps
05	d _ _ _ _ e	The end or death of something
06	a _ _ _ _ _ _ n	A skilled worker who makes things by hand
07	h _ _ _ _ _ s	To utilize or control a resource for a specific purpose
08	g _ _ _ e	Cunning or deceitful behaviour
09	s _ _ _ _ _ _ _ e	To try to obtain something without paying for it
10	c _ _ _ _ _ _ _ t	To show the difference between things
11	f _ _ _ _ _ _ _ _ l	To prevent something by acting in advance
12	o _ _ _ _ _ _ _ e	Stubborn and resistant to change
13	i _ _ _ _ _ _ _ n	A cut made with a sharp tool
14	v _ _ _ _ _ n	A person who has had long experience in a particular field
15	v _ _ _ _ _ e	High quality and lasting value, or representing the best of its kind

WK26	Word	Definition
01	i _ _ _ r	Deduce or conclude information based on evidence
02	b _ _ _ _ _ _ y	Briefness or conciseness
03	i _ _ _ _ _ _ e	Extremely large or vast
04	c _ _ _ x	The most important or difficult part of something
05	t _ _ _ e	A temporary agreement to stop fighting
06	g _ _ _ _ _ _ s	Kind and polite
07	i _ _ _ _ _ _ _ _ e	To suggest someone is involved in a crime
08	g _ _ _ _ _ _ _ _ h	Nonsense words
09	a _ _ _ _ _ _ _ t	Something that's different or unusual
10	a _ _ _ _ _ _ r	Apart or divided into pieces
11	p _ _ _ _ _ _ t	Childishly bad-tempered
12	n _ _ _ _ _ _ _ _ _ e	Try to reach an agreement through discussion
13	s _ _ _ _ _ _ r	Thin and delicate
14	i _ _ _ _ _ _ _ _ e	Something that motivates or encourages action
15	s _ _ _ _ e	Dark, gloomy or depressing

WK27	Word	Definition
01	c _ _ _ _ _ _ _ _ _ n	A strong belief or a guilty verdict in court
02	t _ _ _ _ _ e	Walk slowly with heavy steps
03	f _ _ _ _ e	To handle something clumsily
04	s _ _ _ _ d	Holy; deserving of respect
05	d _ _ _ _ _ _ e	To give orders or command
06	p _ _ _ _ _ _ _ e	Spreading widely
07	c _ _ b	To control or limit something
08	r _ _ _ _ _ _ t	A small remaining piece of something
09	p _ _ _ _ _ e	Be in charge of a meeting or formal event
10	p _ _ _ _ y	Calm someone who is angry or upset
11	i _ _ _ _ _ _ _ _ _ _ l	Happening as a minor part or result of something else
12	p _ _ _ _ _ _ _ _ _ t	Continuing despite difficulties
13	d _ _ _ _ _ _ e	To use up or reduce in quantity
14	b _ _ _ _ _ _ _ d	Surrounded and under attack
15	b _ _ _ _ e	To scold or criticize harshly

WK28	Word	Definition
01	v _ _ _ _ _ _ h	To defeat thoroughly; overcome
02	d _ _ _ _ _ _ _ _ s	In a state of extreme excitement or confusion
03	e _ _ _ _ _ _ y	The ability to understand others' feelings
04	h _ _ d	To pay attention to or take notice of
05	h _ _ _ _ n	To move or act quickly
06	c _ _ _ _ _ _ _ _ _ _ _ _ _ _ e	Communication through letters or emails
07	f _ _ _ _ _ _ _ _ _ _ _ e	In addition to what has already been said
08	m _ _ _ _ d	Damaged or spoiled
09	r _ _ _ _ _ _ _ _ _ _ _ _ n	Recovering from illness or hardship
10	d _ _ _ _ _ _ _ _ e	Destroy severely or cause great emotional pain
11	i _ _ _ _ _ t	Hinder or restrain something
12	d _ _ _ _ _ _ e	Spread out over a wide area
13	c _ _ _ _ _ _ _ _ s	General agreement by a group
14	m _ _ _ _ _ _ _ _ s	Of great importance or significance
15	o _ _ _ e	To flow slowly in a thick, sticky way

WK29	Word	Definition
01	s _ _ _ _ _ _ _ _ t	A feeling or emotion
02	p _ _ _ _ _ _ _ _ t	An earlier event or action that is regarded as an example
03	r _ _ _ _ _ d	Revoke or cancel a decision or order
04	l _ _ _ _ _ _ _ _ _ _ _ _ s	Lack of energy or interest
05	d _ _ _ _ e	Quiet, obedient, and easy to control
06	c _ _ _ _ _ _ _ y	A useful product that can be bought and sold
07	a _ _ _ s	A super deep and dark hole or pit
08	l _ _ _ _ _ _ y	A person who inspires or influences others
09	e _ _ _ _ s	More than what's needed or usual
10	p _ _ _ _ _ e	To make someone less angry or hostile
11	s _ _ _ _ _ _ _ _ t	Unwavering and determined
12	s _ _ _ _ _ _ _ t	Expressed briefly and clearly
13	i _ _ _ _ _ _ _ _ _ s	Arrogant and bossy
14	d _ _ _ _ _ _ _ e	Empty, barren, and deserted
15	a _ _ _ _ _ _ _ _ _ _ _ e	Responsible for what you do

WK30	Word	Definition
01	c _ _ _ t	To desire or wish for something someone else has
02	s _ _ _ _ r	Stay just below the boiling point
03	p _ _ _ _ _ e	Obtain something, especially with effort
04	p _ _ _ _ _ _ _ _ y	The state of being near
05	d _ _ _ _ _ _ _ _ e	Appoint or choose for a specific role
06	e _ _ _ _ _ _ _ _ _ e	Make a problem worse
07	s _ _ _ n	To reject with disdain or contempt
08	p _ _ _ _ _ _ _ _ c	Practical and focused on achieving practical results
09	r _ _ _ _ _ _ _ _ _ e	The refusal to accept or comply with something
10	w _ _ _ e	Give a slight involuntary grimace in response to pain
11	f _ _ _ _ _ _ _ _ _ t	Direct and honest, sometimes bluntly so
12	b _ _ _ _ t	Deprived or lacking something
13	p _ _ _ _ _ _ _ _ _ _ _ s	Inspiring respect and admiration
14	r _ _ _ _ _ _ _ _ _ _ n	Consequence of an action
15	d _ _ _ _ _ _ _ t	Abandoned or in a very poor condition

Test C

WK31	Word	Definition
01	t__ __ __ __ __ __ __t	Lasting only for a short time
02	s__ __ __ __e	To make great efforts to achieve or obtain something
03	n__ __ __e	Having high moral qualities; honourable
04	d__ __ __ __ __ __ __ __e	Worthy of hatred or disgust
05	l__ __t	An rude, badly-behaved person
06	h__ __ __ __ __ __o	Up to this time or point
07	p__ __ __ __ __e	A statement that forms the basis for an argument
08	r__ __t	A crack, split, or break; a serious disagreement
09	a__ __ __ __ __ __n	A strong dislike or disinclination
10	g__ __ __ __ __ __ __e	Easily tricked or deceived
11	s__ __ __k	Bleak, harsh, or bare in appearance
12	t__ __ __ __m	Alongside each other, together
13	e__ __ __ __ __ __ __e	Being subjected to a particular condition or influence
14	d__ __ __ __ __ __ __ __e	Completely different and unrelated
15	c__ __ __ __ __t	Hidden or secretive

WK32	Word	Definition
01	p__ __ __ __ __ __x	A statement that seems contradictory but may be true
02	p__ __ __ __ __ __y	A person with exceptional talent, especially a young one
03	l__ __ __ __ __ __ __ __ __ __e	Domesticated birds raised for meat and eggs
04	p__ __ __ __ __ __ __ __d	Confused or puzzled
05	s__ __ __ __ __ __ __ __ __y	Unity or agreement of feeling
06	i__ __ __ __ __ __ __ __ __ __ __e	Question someone intensely
07	P__ __ __ __ __ __ __ __ __e	Making or creating or achieving a lot
08	a__ __ __ __ __ __ __ __y	Strong feeling of dislike
09	t__ __ __ __t	A cruel and oppressive ruler
10	a__ __ __ __ __ __t	To increase or make something larger
11	p__ __ __ __ __ __ __ __t	Evoking a keen sense of sadness or regret
12	a__ __ __ __ __ __y	A comparison between two things to explain something
13	g__ __ __ __ __ __ __ __e	Shock or excite into taking action
14	c__ __ __ __ __ __e	To travel regularly between home and work
15	p__ __ __ __ __ __ __ __ __ __ __ __n	The act of protecting or maintaining something

Test C

Refer to the corresponding week for answers (pages 1 to 50)

WK33	Word	Definition
01	c _ _ _ _ d	Burned and blackened
02	u _ _ _ _ _ _ _ s	Fully in agreement
03	c _ _ _ _ _ _ _ _ l	Informal language used in everyday conversation
04	s _ _ _ _ _ _ _ _ e	Deceit used to achieve a goal
05	s _ _ _ _ _ r	A place that provides protection from weather or danger
06	f _ _ _ _ _ _ e	Possible, able to be done
07	a _ _ _ t	A feeling of deep anxiety or dread
08	h _ _ _ _ _ y	Arrogant and superior
09	e _ _ _ _ m	Respect and admiration
10	c _ _ _ _ _ _ _ _ _ _ _ _ s	Doing things carefully, wanting to do what's right
11	c _ _ _ _ _ _ _ _ _ _ _ c	Involving a sudden and widespread disaster
12	p _ _ _ _ t	A dangerous or difficult situation
13	e _ _ _ _ _ _ _ e	Make something happen faster
14	r _ _ _ _ _ _ e	Formally give up a right or claim
15	e _ _ _ _ _ e	Reaching a high or the highest degree

WK34	Word	Definition
01	p _ _ _ _ _ _ t	To forbid by law or authority, someone more senior
02	f _ _ _ _ _ t	To lose or give up something as a penalty
03	b _ _ _ _ _ _ d	Charmed or enchanted; sometimes tricked
04	p _ _ _ _ _ _ _ _ s	A set of actions or steps to be followed
05	g _ _ _ _ _ e	A facial expression of pain or disgust
06	a _ _ _ _ _ _ _ _ s	Favourable or bringing good fortune
07	s _ _ _ _ _ _ _ n	The state of being private and away from other people
08	s _ _ _ _ _ _ _ e	To examine or inspect closely and thoroughly
09	t _ _ _ _ h	A long, narrow ditch
10	d _ _ _ e	A flood, or a large amount of something
11	c _ _ _ _ r	To agree or have the same opinion
12	a _ _ _ _ _ e	A collection of historical records or documents
13	b _ _ _ s	Something given as a reward in addition to what is expected
14	p _ _ _ _ _ _ _ e	A special right or advantage
15	i _ _ _ _ _ _ _ e	To intervene or mediate on behalf of others

Test C

Refer to the corresponding week for answers (pages 1 to 50)

WK35	Word	Definition
01	n _ _ _ _ _ _ e	To propose or formally suggest someone for a position
02	i _ _ _ _ _ _ _ _ t	Not showing good judgment, unwise
03	p _ _ _ _ _ _ _ _ _ _ e	To cause something to happen unexpectedly
04	d _ _ _ t	Quick and skilful
05	h _ _ _ _ _ s	Extremely ugly or repulsive
06	m _ _ _ _ e	A chaotic fight or struggle
07	c _ _ _ _ _ _ _ t	Strong dislike or disrespect
08	h _ _ _ _ e	Voice sounding rough and harsh, often due to illness
09	e _ _ _ _ _ e	Difficult to find or define
10	p _ _ _ _ _ _ _ _ n	A large, imposing building
11	i _ _ _ _ _ _ _ _ t	Continuing without stopping, often unpleasantly
12	s _ _ _ _ _ _ _ _ _ _ _ _ _ _ y	At the same time
13	n _ _ _ _ _ _ _ _ y	Being famous for something bad
14	r _ _ _ _ _ _ _ _ _ _ _ e	Complain, protest in a forceful manner
15	c _ _ _ _ _ _ _ _ l	Friendly and pleasant

WK36	Word	Definition
01	h _ _ _ _ _ _ d	Celebrated or announced publicly
02	t _ _ _ _ _ _ _ _ _ _ _ n	Exchange of goods, services, or funds
03	a _ _ _ _ _ _ _ _ _ _ n	A heated or noisy argument or dispute
04	c _ _ _ _ _ s	Large in quantity
05	c _ _ _ _ _ _ _ _ _ _ _ e	Celebrate the memory of someone or something from the past
06	a _ _ _ n	To arrange in a straight line or to support a cause
07	p _ _ _ _ _ _ _ _ _ _ e	Intending to cause a reaction, often anger
08	s _ _ _ _ _ _ _ _ _ _ l	shallow or trivial, not significant
09	c _ _ _ _ _ _ _ _ _ _ _ _ _ n	Statements or ideas that oppose each other
10	r _ _ _ _ d	Having a rough, irregular, or uneven surface
11	c _ _ _ _ _ _ _ _ _ _ n	Sympathy and desire to help those suffering
12	s _ _ _ _ _ _ b	To give in to pressure, temptation, or a negative force
13	a _ _ _ y	Off course or not going as planned
14	a _ _ _ _ _ _ _ m	To get used to something over time
15	c _ _ _ _ _ _ _ a	Personal charm that inspires others

Test C

Refer to the corresponding week for answers (pages 1 to 50)

WK37	Word	Definition
01	c _ _ _ _ _ _ _ _ _ n	Something given up, usually in an argument
02	a _ _ _ _ _ _ _ c	Concerned with beauty and art
03	a _ _ _ _ _ e	Friendly and easy to talk to
04	t _ _ _ _ _ _ _ y	An inclination towards a particular type of thing or action
05	a _ _ _ _ _ e	Negative or unfavourable
06	s _ _ _ _ _ _ s	False or fake
07	e _ _ _ _ _ _ g	Requiring a great deal of care, effort, or precision
08	s _ _ _ _ _ _ t	Not flowing and often having an unpleasant smell as a consequence
09	r _ _ _ _ _ _ _ _ _ e	Ability to recover from difficulties
10	i _ _ _ _ _ _ _ _ _ e	Unable to read or write
11	s _ _ _ _ _ _ r	Waste (money, time, etc.) in a reckless manner
12	t _ _ _ _ _ _ _ _ _ _ _ t	Allowing light, but not detailed shapes, to pass through; semi-transparent
13	g _ _ _ _ _ _ _ s	Attractive in an exciting and special way
14	d _ _ _ _ _ _ _ _ y	A lack of something necessary
15	r _ _ _ _ _ _ _ _ _ e	Belonging or relating separately to each of two or more people or things

WK38	Word	Definition
01	c _ _ _ _ _ l	To reduce or limit
02	a _ _ _ _ _ _ _ n	Divide and share out
03	r _ _ _ _ _ _ _ _ _ _ _ _ _ s	Negative unintended consequences of an action
04	c _ _ p	To hold something tightly
05	s _ _ _ _ _ h	Cautious or secretive movement
06	i _ _ _ _ _ c	Extremely pleasant, peaceful, or picturesque
07	a _ _ _ _ _ _ _ s	Hard-working and diligent
08	s _ _ _ _ _ _ _ _ _ l	Large in amount, size or importance
09	s _ _ e	The range or size of the area or topic
10	s _ g	Sink, droop, or settle from weight or pressure
11	f _ _ _ _ r	Hesitate or stumble, lose momentum
12	p _ _ _ _ _ _ _ _ s	Having developed abilities at an earlier age than usual
13	s _ _ _ _ _ _ t	Harsh, loud, and grating
14	a _ _ _ s	Gather together a large quantity
15	r _ _ _ _ _ _ _ t	No longer needed or useful

WK39	Word	Definition
01	f __ __ __ __ l	Thrifty, careful with money
02	p __ __ __ __ __ __ e	To sweat
03	c __ __ __ __ __ e	Put together information from different places
04	a __ __ __ __ __ __ __ s	Bold or daring in a fearless way
05	p __ __ __ __ __ e	To come before in time or order
06	t __ __ __ __ __ h	A great victory or achievement
07	v __ __ __ __ __ __ n	A person's employment or main occupation
08	s __ __ __ __ __ __ __ y	A place of refuge or safety
09	g __ __ __ __ e	Distort or mix up, making unclear
10	q __ __ __ __ __ __ e	A difficult, complex situation OR soft wet area of land that gives away
11	t __ __ __ __ e	A long angry speech
12	s __ __ __ __ __ e	Cheat to obtain money fraudulently
13	t __ __ __ __ __ s	Too long, slow, or dull; tiresome or monotonous
14	b __ __ __ __ __ n	To grow or flourish rapidly
15	i __ __ __ __ __ __ __ __ __ __ __ __ e	Done randomly, without careful selection

WK40	Word	Definition
01	d __ __ __ __ r	To be indecisive or uncertain
02	b __ __ __ __ __ __ e	Blunt or abrupt in speech or manner
03	p __ __ __ __ __ __ __ e	The highest point or peak of achievement
04	b __ __ __ __ __ __ g	Deeply thoughtful, often in a moody or gloomy way
05	p __ __ __ __ __ __ __ __ __ __ __ s	Absurd, ridiculous
06	a __ __ __ t	To turn away or prevent
07	r __ __ __ __ __ __ __ __ t	Unwilling and hesitant
08	C __ __ __ __ __ __ __ __ e	Helping something to happen, making it easier
09	e __ __ __ __ __ __ __ __ __ __ t	Bubbly and lively, like sparkling water
10	i __ __ __ __ e	Persuade, or cause something to happen
11	h __ __ __ __ __ __ s	Showing a reckless lack of attention
12	c __ __ __ __ __ __ __ y	The maximum amount that something can hold or produce
13	c __ __ __ __ __ __ __ d	Scolded or criticized severely
14	p __ __ __ __ __ __ __ t	Important or well-known
15	d __ __ __ __ __ __ __ e	To assign tasks or responsibilities to others

Test C

Refer to the corresponding week for answers (pages 1 to 50)

WK41	Word	Definition
01	f__ __ __ __ __ __ __ __ t	Bold, colourful, and showy
02	i__ __ __ t	Lacking skill or ability
03	t__ __ __ __ __ __ y	Careful about spending money
04	e__ __ __ __ __ __ __ a	Extreme happiness
05	s__ __ __ __ __ __ __ s	Forcibly put an end to
06	d__ __ __ __ __ __ __ __ __ e	To make someone or something weak
07	a__ __ __ __ __ __ __ __ __ __ __ c	Showing active opposition or hostility
08	i__ __ __ __ e	To enter forcefully or intrude
09	p__ __ __ __ __ __ t	A strong liking or preference for something
10	b__ __ __ __ n	To express grief or disappointment
11	e__ __ __ t	Praise or think very highly of
12	c__ __ __ __ __ __ __ __ __ d	Complicated and difficult to understand
13	c__ __ __ __ __ __ e	To interpret or understand
14	c__ __ __ __ __ __ __ __ __ y	Doing something the same way over time
15	c__ __ __ __ __ __ e	Deserving blame or responsibility

WK42	Word	Definition
01	f__ __ __ __ __ __ c	Fast, energetic, and uncontrolled
02	f__ __ x	Artificial or imitation; not genuine.
03	s__ __ __ __ __ __ e	Friendly and enjoys being with other people
04	t__ __ __ __ __ __ __ __ e	Unsure or uncertain
05	p__ __ __ __ __ __ __ d	Extremely frightened
06	c__ __ __ __ __ __ __ __ __ s	Easily noticeable or standing out
07	c__ __ __ __ __ __ __ __ __ e	To confirm or support
08	c__ __ __ __ __ __ __ y	The state of being imprisoned or confined
09	d__ __ __ __ __ __ t	Hard-working and careful
10	b__ __ __ __ __ c	Savage or brutal in behaviour
11	q__ __ __ __ __ y	A dilemma, a difficult choice
12	z__ __ __ __ h	The highest point or state
13	a__ __ __ __ __ __ e	A special award or praise
14	f__ __ __ __ __ __ y	Excessive or insincere praise
15	w__ __ __ __ __ __ d	Very unhappy or in poor condition

WK43	Word	Definition
01	v _ _ _ _ _ _ _ _ e	Having a strong desire for revenge
02	c _ _ _ _ _ _ _ _ _ _ y	Modern or current
03	s _ _ _ _ _ y	Strong and robust; able to withstand rough handling
04	i _ _ _ _ r	To weaken or damage
05	r _ _ _ _ _ _ _ _ _ _ n	Punishment inflicted as vengeance for a wrong
06	v _ _ _ _ e	Capable of working or surviving
07	i _ _ _ _ _ _ _ _ _ t	Having no interest or concern
08	i _ _ _ _ _ _ _ s	Clever and original
09	p _ _ _ p	Rounded, slightly fat
10	c _ _ _ _ _ _ _ _ _ _ e	Friendship and trust between people
11	f _ _ _ _ _ _ _ _ _ _ s	Imaginary, not real
12	c _ _ _ _ _ e	To accept or allow something even if wrong
13	c _ _ _ _ _ _ _ _ _ _ _ _ e	Including all or many details
14	u _ _ _ _ _ h	Lacking good manners or refinement
15	s _ _ _ _ _ e	Become less intense or violent

WK44	Word	Definition
01	d _ _ _ _ _ _ _ _ _ g	Saying mean things that make someone or something seem not as good.
02	p _ _ _ _ _ _ s	Full of danger or risk; hazardous.
03	c _ _ _ _ _ t	Satisfied, not wanting more
04	c _ _ _ _ _ _ _ _ t	Having the necessary ability or skill
05	d _ _ _ _ _ e	To strongly disapprove or regret
06	c _ _ _ _ _ _ _ _ _ _ _ n	Protecting and preserving natural resources
07	e _ _ _ _ t	To strongly encourage or urge someone to do something
08	c _ _ _ _ _ _ _ _ _ _ n	Payment to make up for loss or injury
09	i _ _ _ _ _ _ _ _ _ e	Absolutely necessary or crucial
10	b _ _ _ _ _ _ _ _ _ d	Beset (attack from all sides) with hardship and difficulties
11	e _ _ _ _ _ _ _ e	Clear someone of blame or guilt
12	r _ _ _ _ _ _ _ _ h	To fill or make complete again
13	p _ _ _ _ _ _ _ _ s	Successful and wealthy
14	a _ _ _ _ _ _ _ y	Strong dislike or hostility
15	f _ _ _ _ _ _ _ _ s	Happening by chance or luck

Test C

Refer to the corresponding week for answers (pages 1 to 50)

WK45	Word	Definition
01	E _ _ _ _ _ _ y	A moment of sudden and great revelation or realization.
02	e _ _ _ _ _ _ _ c	Difficult to understand, mysterious, or puzzling.
03	r _ _ _ _ _ _ _ d	A formal expression of disapproval
04	r _ _ _ _ _ e	Worsen again after a period of improvement
05	a _ _ _ _ _ _ _ _ _ c	Extremely angry or furious
06	s _ _ _ _ _ _ _ _ _ _ e	Provide evidence to support a claim
07	s _ _ _ _ _ t	A portion or part of something
08	c _ _ _ _ _ _ _ _ _ _ g	Holding attention in a fascinating way
09	r _ _ _ _ m	Make changes to improve something
10	p _ _ _ _ _ _ _ e	Believable or reasonable
11	b _ _ e	Something causing misery or annoyance
12	b _ _ _ _ _ _ _ _ _ _ y	Many rules and regulations
13	i _ _ _ _ _ _ _ _ _ _ s	Unwilling or unable to believe something
14	t _ _ _ _ _ l	A state of great disturbance, confusion, or uncertainty
15	s _ _ _ _ _ _ y	A long-term plan of action

WK46	Word	Definition
01	o _ _ _ _ s	Extremely unpleasant or repulsive
02	C _ _ _ _ _ _ _ _ e	Staying calm and controlled
03	b _ _ _ _ _ _ _ _ _ t	Well-meaning and kindly
04	f _ _ _ _ _ _ _ _ _ _ g	Ready to help, or happening soon
05	o _ _ _ _ _ _ e	Wealth and luxury
06	r _ _ _ _ l	A religious or solemn ceremony; established routine
07	p _ _ _ _ _ _ _ _ _ _ g	Treating others in a condescending way
08	c _ _ _ _ _ _ e	Feeling remorse or guilt
09	l _ _ _ _ d	Highly praised or celebrated
10	w _ _ _ _ _ _ w	Remove or take away; retreat
11	h _ _ _ t	Lift or raise something up, usually with ropes
12	d _ _ _ _ _ _ _ _ _ _ _ _ e	Show the difference between things
13	i _ _ _ _ _ _ _ _ _ l	Showing deep understanding of something
14	e _ _ _ _ t	Free from an obligation others must obey
15	d _ _ _ _ _ _ _ e	To gradually disappear or scatter

Test C

WK47	Word	Definition
01	t _ _ _ _ _ _ _ _ t	Equivalent in seriousness to; virtually the same as
02	i _ _ _ _ _ e	To beg desperately
03	d _ _ _ _ _ _ _ _ _ _ e	Spread information widely
04	d _ _ _ _ e	Shy, modest
05	p _ _ _ _ _ e	To assume, especially without strong evidence
06	i _ _ _ _ _ o	A large and dangerous fire
07	i _ _ _ _ _ _ _ _ _ _ d	Extremely poor
08	d _ _ _ _ _ _ _ _ _ l	Harmful or damaging
09	u _ _ _ _ _ _ _ _ _ l	leaving no doubt - clear
10	c _ _ _ _ _ _ _ _ e	To be the parts that form something
11	a _ _ _ _ _ _ _ n	To find out or make certain
12	t _ _ _ _ _ _ _ y	A river or stream flowing into a larger river or lake
13	t _ _ _ _ d	Very hot and dry; passionate
14	c _ _ _ _ _ _ _ d	Jointly arranged or planned
15	a _ _ _ _ _ _ _ _ e	To make something shorter or use fewer letters

WK48	Word	Definition
01	o _ _ _ _ _ _ _ _ e	To destroy completely
02	c _ _ _ _ _ _ _ _ _ t	A person or thing similar to another
03	i _ _ _ _ _ e	Copy the behaviour or appearance of someone or something
04	p _ _ _ _ _ _ _ d	Having deep meaning or significance
05	d _ _ _ _ _ f	To question or provide information after an event
06	f _ _ _ _ _ _ _ _ _ _ _ _ y	At the most basic level
07	r _ _ _ _ _ _ e	Repeat to emphasize
08	C _ _ _ _ _ _ e	To nurture or develop
09	t _ _ _ t	A distinguishing characteristic or quality
10	f _ _ _ _ _ _ y	Extreme fierceness or aggressiveness
11	g _ _ _ _ _ t	Brave and noble
12	h _ _ _ e	To lift or throw something with great effort
13	d _ _ _ t	A storage place for goods or vehicles
14	d _ _ _ _ y	Sleepy
15	p _ _ _ e	To investigate closely

Test C

Refer to the corresponding week for answers (pages 1 to 50)

WK49	Word	Definition
01	m _ _ _ _ _ _ _ _ _ _ _ _ s	Made up of a variety of unrelated things
02	a _ _ _ _ _ e	To make something less severe or intense
03	e _ _ _ _ _ _ _ _ y	Serving as an excellent example or model
04	d _ _ _ _ s	Threats or pressure forcing someone to do something
05	p _ _ _ _ _ _ _ _ _ _ e	Visually striking (like a beautiful landscape)
06	c _ _ _ _ _ e	A series of things that happen quickly and often with a domino effect
07	f _ _ _ _ _ _ _ s	Silly and not serious
08	t _ _ _ _ g	Difficult or demanding
09	p _ _ _ _ _ _ l	Having the possibility to develop into something
10	i _ _ _ _ _ m	in between two time points, temporary
11	p _ _ _ _ _ l	Win or succeed, especially after a struggle
12	r _ _ _ _ _ _ _ e	Demote to a lower position
13	v _ _ _ y	Speak or write about in an abusively disparaging manner
14	d _ _ _ k	To prove a claim false
15	a _ _ _ _ _ _ _ _ _ _ e	The design and structure of buildings

WK50	Word	Definition
01	e _ _ _ _ _ _ e	To increase rapidly or intensify
02	d _ _ _ _ e	To damage someone's reputation with false statements
03	m _ _ _ _ a	A harbour for small boats or yachts
04	f _ _ _ _ _ _ _ _ g	A sense or feeling that something bad will happen
05	i _ _ _ _ _ _ e	Deceptive or difficult to find
06	c _ _ _ _ _ _ _ _ _ _ y	Trying to make peace
07	a _ _ _ _ _ c	Very old and outdated
08	c _ _ _ t	Power or influence
09	s _ _ _ _ _ e	A miserly person
10	p _ _ _ _ _ c	Producing a lot of something
11	h _ _ _ _ _ _ _ _ _ _ l	Saying one thing but doing the opposite
12	d _ _ _ l	Cause something (like a train or conversation) to go off track
13	C _ _ _ _ _ _ _ _ _ n	Sad and disappointed
14	c _ _ _ c	A person who doubts the sincerity of others
15	l _ _ e	To rent or let temporarily

TEST LOG

Record the result of each week's test to track progress
and ensure words are not forgotten over time!

Test No.	Test A	Test B	Test C	Notes
1				
2				
3				
4				
5				
6				
7				
8				
9				
10				
11				
12				
13				
14				
15				
16				
17				
18				
19				
20				
21				
22				
23				
24				
25				

TEST LOG

Record the result of each week's test to track progress and ensure words are not forgotten over time!

Test No.	Test A	Test B	Test C	Notes
26				
27				
28				
29				
30				
31				
32				
33				
34				
35				
36				
37				
38				
39				
40				
41				
42				
43				
44				
45				
46				
47				
48				
49				
50				

Answers

Puzzle of the Week - Answers

WK #	Answer	WK #	Answer
1	Postpone	26	Truce
2	anguish	27	berate
3	stern	28	heed
4	dearth	29	placate
5	duplicity	30	spurn
6	benign	31	aversion
7	pedantic	32	galvanise
8	chronological	33	expedite
9	solitude	34	intercede
10	truant	35	elusive
11	exuberance	36	provocative
12	wither	37	glamorous
13	improvise	38	precocious
14	surveillance	39	sanctuary
15	verbose	40	heedless
16	placid	41	euphoria
17	complicity	42	barbaric
18	voracious	43	contemporary
19	pompous	44	imperative
20	ruthless	45	bureaucracy
21	pretence	46	contrite
22	dilapidated	47	abbreviate
23	sumptuous	48	gallant
24	stalwart	49	frivolous
25	scrounge	50	conciliatory

WK 01	1	2	3	4	5	6	7	8	9	10	11	12	13	14	15
	I	C	O	F	H	K	A	G	L	D	E	J	M	B	N

WK 02	1	2	3	4	5	6	7	8	9	10	11	12	13	14	15
	J	N	F	A	L	I	K	C	M	H	D	G	O	E	B

WK 03	1	2	3	4	5	6	7	8	9	10	11	12	13	14	15
	M	L	K	J	B	D	N	A	C	O	E	F	G	I	H

WK 04	1	2	3	4	5	6	7	8	9	10	11	12	13	14	15
	E	M	N	H	B	O	F	A	K	C	D	J	L	G	I

WK 05	1	2	3	4	5	6	7	8	9	10	11	12	13	14	15
	G	A	N	C	O	F	J	B	L	M	H	K	I	D	E

WK 06	1	2	3	4	5	6	7	8	9	10	11	12	13	14	15
	O	E	N	C	B	G	F	H	D	A	I	L	M	J	K

WK 07	1	2	3	4	5	6	7	8	9	10	11	12	13	14	15
	K	E	H	O	F	J	L	B	A	D	C	M	I	G	N

WK 08	1	2	3	4	5	6	7	8	9	10	11	12	13	14	15
	L	O	B	F	H	N	A	J	K	M	G	D	I	E	C

WK 09	1	2	3	4	5	6	7	8	9	10	11	12	13	14	15
	L	N	E	A	K	D	C	J	M	I	G	B	O	F	H

WK 10	1	2	3	4	5	6	7	8	9	10	11	12	13	14	15
	J	D	C	H	F	M	B	I	O	G	E	L	A	N	K

WK 11	1	2	3	4	5	6	7	8	9	10	11	12	13	14	15
	D	J	H	A	G	E	B	O	I	F	M	C	N	K	L

WK 12	1	2	3	4	5	6	7	8	9	10	11	12	13	14	15
	L	F	B	M	O	K	N	A	I	E	G	H	J	D	C

WK 13	1	2	3	4	5	6	7	8	9	10	11	12	13	14	15
	I	L	K	C	M	G	O	E	D	A	N	B	J	F	H

WK 14	1	2	3	4	5	6	7	8	9	10	11	12	13	14	15
	M	G	A	B	D	J	K	F	E	L	C	I	N	O	H

WK 15	1	2	3	4	5	6	7	8	9	10	11	12	13	14	15
	F	I	C	D	O	N	K	J	H	A	E	G	B	M	L

WK 16	1	2	3	4	5	6	7	8	9	10	11	12	13	14	15
	K	H	E	L	M	G	C	I	B	N	D	J	O	F	A

WK 17	1	2	3	4	5	6	7	8	9	10	11	12	13	14	15
	M	B	D	I	G	J	L	N	E	H	C	K	F	A	O

WK 18	1	2	3	4	5	6	7	8	9	10	11	12	13	14	15
	B	J	M	C	N	G	K	L	D	I	E	A	O	H	F

WK 19	1	2	3	4	5	6	7	8	9	10	11	12	13	14	15
	J	C	A	M	O	K	F	G	B	L	N	D	I	E	H

WK 20	1	2	3	4	5	6	7	8	9	10	11	12	13	14	15
	G	B	E	N	I	J	F	M	K	O	C	L	A	H	D

WK 21	1	2	3	4	5	6	7	8	9	10	11	12	13	14	15
	B	C	G	J	O	K	L	E	A	F	M	H	I	D	N

WK 22	1	2	3	4	5	6	7	8	9	10	11	12	13	14	15
	I	O	N	E	D	C	G	A	H	B	J	M	L	K	F

WK 23	1	2	3	4	5	6	7	8	9	10	11	12	13	14	15
	N	J	G	H	M	B	C	L	F	O	I	K	D	A	E

WK 24	1	2	3	4	5	6	7	8	9	10	11	12	13	14	15
	G	H	F	I	A	L	J	C	M	O	N	E	K	D	B

Test B Answers

WK	1	2	3	4	5	6	7	8	9	10	11	12	13	14	15
25	I	M	C	D	G	B	L	H	F	K	O	E	N	A	J

WK	1	2	3	4	5	6	7	8	9	10	11	12	13	14	15
26	B	J	H	K	L	G	N	E	O	I	C	D	A	M	F

WK	1	2	3	4	5	6	7	8	9	10	11	12	13	14	15
27	L	E	I	J	G	H	F	B	N	O	K	A	C	D	M

WK	1	2	3	4	5	6	7	8	9	10	11	12	13	14	15
28	I	J	C	D	L	K	B	O	N	F	E	G	M	H	A

WK	1	2	3	4	5	6	7	8	9	10	11	12	13	14	15
29	I	N	K	L	F	O	M	A	E	J	G	D	C	B	H

WK	1	2	3	4	5	6	7	8	9	10	11	12	13	14	15
30	O	F	K	G	L	E	N	B	H	A	M	D	J	C	I

WK	1	2	3	4	5	6	7	8	9	10	11	12	13	14	15
31	J	I	A	D	L	C	K	B	F	G	N	M	O	E	H

WK	1	2	3	4	5	6	7	8	9	10	11	12	13	14	15
32	C	D	I	L	K	O	B	A	E	N	H	F	M	J	G

WK	1	2	3	4	5	6	7	8	9	10	11	12	13	14	15
33	G	J	N	K	I	A	O	E	L	M	H	C	B	F	D

WK	1	2	3	4	5	6	7	8	9	10	11	12	13	14	15
34	L	B	K	O	A	E	D	M	N	J	G	H	C	I	F

WK	1	2	3	4	5	6	7	8	9	10	11	12	13	14	15
35	J	F	L	O	M	C	I	B	K	G	H	A	E	D	N

WK	1	2	3	4	5	6	7	8	9	10	11	12	13	14	15
36	O	E	M	N	F	D	C	I	A	B	J	H	L	G	K

WK	1	2	3	4	5	6	7	8	9	10	11	12	13	14	15
37	B	A	F	G	O	K	J	M	N	E	I	C	L	D	H

WK	1	2	3	4	5	6	7	8	9	10	11	12	13	14	15
38	K	B	L	M	E	H	O	N	J	I	G	A	D	C	F
39	M	C	F	L	J	G	H	D	N	I	A	O	B	E	K
40	O	L	M	N	K	D	F	H	B	E	I	A	J	C	G
41	M	J	I	F	A	K	O	D	B	N	L	H	C	G	E
42	D	E	O	A	G	F	M	B	C	N	J	K	L	H	I
43	D	E	O	L	K	A	B	N	G	C	M	F	H	J	I
44	C	D	F	A	O	I	M	B	H	L	N	G	J	K	E
45	L	E	J	F	O	K	B	I	M	D	N	C	G	A	H
46	E	G	K	L	N	H	F	I	D	M	J	A	O	C	B
47	I	K	N	H	L	J	E	O	M	C	D	A	F	G	B
48	F	J	H	O	N	I	D	L	G	B	C	E	K	A	M
49	E	I	G	A	H	D	J	K	O	B	C	N	L	M	F
50	I	C	O	F	H	K	A	G	L	D	E	J	M	B	N